# A MATTER OF
# CHOICE

DENA MICHELLI & JULIE SIMPSON

# A MATTER OF
# CHOICE

## A COMPANION FOR MAKING EVERYDAY
## OR LIFE-CHANGING CHOICES

**Marshall Cavendish**
Business

Cover design: Opalworks Co Ltd

Copyright © 2011 Marshall Cavendish International
Published by Marshall Cavendish Business
An imprint of Marshall Cavendish International

PO Box 65829
London EC1P 1NY
United Kingdom
info@marshallcavendish.co.uk

and

1 New Industrial Road
Singapore 536196
genrefsales@sg.marshallcavendish.com
www.marshallcavendish.com/genref

Marshall Cavendish is a trademark of Times Publishing Limited

Other Marshall Cavendish offices:
Marshall Cavendish Corporation. 99 White Plains Road, Tarrytown NY 10591–
9001, USA • Marshall Cavendish International (Thailand) Co Ltd. 253 Asoke,
12th Floor, Sukhumvit 21 Road, Klongtoey Nua, Wattana, Bangkok 10110,
Thailand • Marshall Cavendish (Malaysia) Sdn Bhd, Times Subang, Lot 46,
Subang Hi-Tech Industrial Park, Batu Tiga, 40000 Shah Alam, Selangor Darul
Ehsan, Malaysia

A CIP record for this book is available from the British Library

ISBN 978-981-4328-07-4

Printed and bound in Great Britain by TJ International

# Contents

# A Matter of Thanks

We came to write this book with tremendous enthusiasm and a clear view of what we were hoping to achieve – that is, to enable people to live to their full potential through making their own meaningful choices. This is a big vision and we could not have approached it without the generosity and commitment of those who have supported us throughout the project.

Firstly, Jeremy Kourdi, a remarkable and prolific writer himself, put us in touch with Martin Liu, our commissioner from Marshall Cavendish. Martin was inspired and motivated by our idea and ensured that the publishing vehicle, from concept to delivery, was expectant and well-oiled. His encouragement and support has been persistent and he has been a timely and expert guide.

Our storytellers, to whom we have guaranteed anonymity, have been amazing. Not only in their willingness to share some of their most momentous choices, but also in their belief and commitment to this work. They know who they are, and to them all we would like to say a huge 'thank you'. You are the backbone of this book and your voices will make a difference, for sure, to the readers who will be inspired by your example to make great choices.

Both of us would like to thank our nearest and dearest for providing 'a safe place' for us to work. Their dogged belief in us and tolerance of the change in life's rhythm, which we imposed upon them, has made all the difference. So, Rob and John, thank you.

We sincerely hope that this book will be a good companion to you.

*Dena Michelli and Julie Simpson*
*Spring 2011*

# CHAPTER 1

# **Introduction**

- *Do you have the confidence to make the choices you wish to make?*
- *Do you feel equipped to achieve your dreams and aspirations?*
- *Are you able to tap your full potential to live a happy and satisfying life?*

If you are holding this book, you may well be asking yourself such questions – and we'd like to help you answer them. We will not be answering them for you, however. We are not experts in your life and we are not here to tell you what to do. We are here because we understand the ebb and flow of choice-making as witnesses and facilitators, and we'd like to share with you the things we have learned along with the experiences of others. We are also here because, like everyone else, we are practitioners who try to make the best choices possible. When we get it right, we believe it is due to the quality of the choice-making process we have followed. We believe, too, that this process can always be improved and enhanced. When it is, it will lead to better choices, better outcomes and better lives.

**This is not a book about the choices we make; it is a book about how we make choices.**

Choice is about deciding between many possibilities, picking from a variety of options, selecting a preference. Making decisions commits us to a certain path, a path that says something about us. As social beings, we care about how we are seen by others – often too much and at great cost to ourselves. As we show who we are through our choices, we can feel exposed and sometimes vulnerable, being open to criticism or ridicule.

## Choices and Change

Choices lead to change. Change takes us into the unknown, and it is in this strange and uncertain place that we reveal ourselves in our judgements. Ironically, it is precisely when we are at our most unsure that the quality of our decisions are most visible! The feeling of isolation in our choosing and the fear of 'getting it wrong' may dissuade us from making progress and render us stuck. What is more, the lure of the familiar will often seduce us into staying with the 'devil we know' rather than risk making those hard and unpredictable decisions that will take us into the unknown.

In the film, *The Bridges of Madison County*, Meryl Steep says: 'We are the choices that we have made.' Every choice that we have made in the past has brought us to where we are today. One choice leads to another and creates our life edifice. This means that each choice carries significance, however major or minor. This is both the blessing and curse of choosing.

Choosing, however hard, presents us with opportunities to use qualities that may never before have seen the light of day. As we practice choosing and as our talent as choice makers becomes more conscious and robust, it will be as if we are weaving together the gold and silver threads of confidence that will carry us into a truly autonomous future. In this way, choices present us with the opportunity to emerge in our fullness. Choices lead us into daring and exciting territory. Choices bring us to life!

Choices range from those we make daily ('Shall I have another chocolate?') to those that affect our lives ('Shall I take this job?'). With so many pressures and influences to take into account, the options can quickly become complex and confusing. Getting lost in this confusion is not only uncomfortable but it can also stultify our ability to find a direction and move forward. Sometimes we languish in our dilemmas for years or a lifetime. Sometimes we make decisions in haste. Sometimes our haste leads to regrets. Sometimes we get happy, really happy. Sometimes we just sit, stuck! Making choices can change our lives; it is a creative art that enables us to express our true personalities, values and beliefs and make great use of our experiences.

Humans are dynamic beings made up of fragile and delicate psychological systems that ensure any sense of permanence is an illusion. As a result, we need to review our position constantly and check that we are on the path that is most conducive to our sense of achievement and happiness. Yet, as most of us seek stability and certainty, we will not be inclined to do this; nor will those around us, who collude in the perpetuation of the status quo. This can box us in uncomfortably, and stop us from accessing our personality and creativity at a more subtle level. It follows that unless we can attune ourselves to the fine rhythms of our lives and have the courage of our convictions (sometimes against the interests of those close to us), we will not become well-informed choice makers. Instead, we'll remain as blunt instruments that sabotage real choice.

There is a lot of colour and richness in being an individual and living life in a unique way, yet we are not schooled in self-expression. In our formative years, we are trained to co-operate and fall in step with the crowd. If we dare to show our idiosyncrasies, we may experience being pilloried and encouraged back into our box – for ease of management, perhaps! It does take a fair degree of courage and persistence, therefore, to find and differentiate ourselves as we become adults. But when we become attuned to our own personalities, we can express our potential fully and without apology. This means making clear, concise and honest choices. It is OK to be different – there is no such thing as a universally good or right person, and there's no such thing as a universally good or right choice!

## Self-Awareness and Self-Commitment

The path to developing the art of choice is not necessarily an easy one, although some may be blessed with a natural gift in this department! There are times when you need to reflect on your choices by yourself and there are times when input from others is valuable. Both these avenues lead to self-awareness, the touchstone for good choice-making. In this book we suggest not only that you ask yourself good questions and challenge your self-perception, but also that you get others' opinions and feedback. Often, those close to us see our potential more clearly than we do ourselves and can encourage us to take the kind of chances that we might not take from our own volition. Accepting the possibility that you have more potential than you originally thought – whether you believe it or not – will open up new worlds and fresh territory in which to make bold choices.

Choice-making demands courage because it reveals your willingness to take responsibility for yourself and claim your rightful place in the world. Making a public commitment to your own talents and aspirations might feel like setting yourself up for the tough knocks of criticism and judgement that could follow. But out of this self-commitment come the innate green shoots of great choice-making. There are always those who feel that your success threatens theirs, that it is a zero sum game and there is not enough to go around! But those who care for you will encourage you to be everything you can be and will support you in your intentions. So we're saying, 'Go for it!' Better to have tried and failed than not to have tried at all!

Once you develop the skills of choice-making, it is a generative process: you begin to understand what needs to be done, and once over the initial inertia of resistance, the process becomes self-reinforcing, allowing you to be bolder and brighter in the choices you make. Rather like running on well-oiled wheels, the road becomes smoother – it still has chicanes, cambers and potholes, but you know how to negotiate them with more awareness and skill. Your ability to harness your power and make choices for yourself rests, we believe, on the extent of your self-understanding and self-belief.

Our ability to become great choice makers is contingent upon us being able to employ both the practical and the instinctual side of our beings. The practical side allows us to think clearly, which may involve analyzing the reasons and implications of our choices. The instinctual side is more engaged in listening to our intuition, which may involve taking chances and doing something new or unusual. There is another element too: that of conceiving and reaching for our dreams. This is the powerhouse of our choice making. If we are going to combine these attributes effectively, we need to understand and trust ourselves well.

Ensuring that we have someone with whom we can execute a reality check may be important if we are to make the 'right' choices for ourselves. This is someone who is on our side and willing to perform the range of tasks, from validation to contradiction, encouragement to opposition, staying and leaving; a true companion. It is the importance of this sense of companionship that gave birth to this book.

## A Book about Choice-Making

In our professional lives as coaches, we work with people who are continually faced with choices. They wrestle with them; they seek ways of analysing them; they try to understand them; they worry about them. They make their choices and, even then, they often despair of them. Our job is to help these people illuminate the truth of their dilemma so they can make choices that feel authentic, that speak of their passion and purpose and not of others' expectation or compromise.

At the risk of sounding indiscriminate, this book is aimed at everyone, as everyone has to make choices. Our approach has been to find and share true stories of choice in the words of those who have made them. We have included stories from children as well as a wide age-range of adults who have made every-day as well as life-changing choices. Together, our contributors reflect on things that worked, as well as on things they might have chosen to do differently if they had their time again. The stories include some good ideas and much common sense, and reveal the personal qualities necessary to become a good choice maker.

Listening to other people's stories and understanding what they did and why they did it, we think, is a fabulous way to learn. However, forcing someone else's solution to fit your own particular situation denies autonomous choice and deflects the responsibility for making it. So, we ask you not to replicate others' solutions, but to take inspiration from the stories in this book and understand them within the context of your own life. When you read the stories, ask yourself, 'What would I have done in the same circumstances?' Or, 'What would have prevented me from acting in the way that they did?' In your life, can you see patterns where you have done the same thing over and over again to limit yourself? Notice the difference between your patterns and that of the storyteller's; what does it show you about yourself?

Our patterns are created and adopted because they enable us to survive, so they are not necessarily negative and you may want to keep some of them. However, in the changing circumstances of your life, there are probably patterns that are no longer relevant or helpful. In which case, you might want to change them. This may be as simple as saying, 'I'm not going to do this anymore!' Or, 'I'm going to do something different now!' Whatever tactic you employ, once you are aware of the situations in which you usually play out your patterns, you will be able to stop yourself from doing so.

In addition to the stories we have put together a 'toolkit', which includes our storytellers' tips and techniques, as well as some of our own.

## Tools and Resources

Acknowledging that everyone has a unique way of learning and adopting new ideas, we have approached our toolkit from three directions:

- The first is **conceptual**, for those who like to have a framework for thinking about things.
- The second is **inquisitorial**, for those who like to be challenged and pushed into unfamiliar ground.
- The third is **practical**, for those who like to identify the potential means of moving forward.

We encourage you to put the pieces together in a way that suits your needs and have the most impact. There is no question that some of the approaches take practice, but there is also no question that if you stick at them, they work.

It is our intention that this book will be a thoughtful and honest exploration of the subject of choice and that it will demystify the process of informed choice-making. We sincerely hope that it will enable you to mine the riches of your own wisdom and not look outside yourself for solutions and resolutions. We'd like it to mean that you assemble a portable, internal resource that is available every time a choice needs to be made, however extreme it may feel. And we'd like this book to help you develop trust in yourself as the arbiter of your own destiny.

We also hope our relationship with you as a companion will be long term. This means that whatever difficulties you face in your life, however tough your choices become, you will find courage and inspiration from the stories, thoughts and ideas and the practical solutions found in this book.

If everyone improved his or her choice-making skill by a meagre 10 per cent, what a different world we would live in. More creativity. More fun. More ingenuity. Not only would this be an extraordinary feat for an individual, but also, we would ensure that we passed our children a valuable inheritance and a rich culture in which they could make their own choices.

We wanted to write this book to enable people to take charge of their lives in an ongoing and developing way, to raise awareness of their own capability and potentiality as pilots of their own life journey. Although we realise this is a big agenda, we wanted the plethora of ideas and techniques that emerge from the stories to be compelling, so that you can develop a life skill that frees you to be all that you can be. This aim is ambitious enough, but we have a bigger dream, too; that is, to trigger a wave of positive, creative and expansive energy through the exercise of bold, integrated choices. In our experience, when we become responsible and confident in our choosing, we become less preoccupied with ourselves and more concerned about how we can contribute to the unfolding problems of the world, where there is so much work to be done.

CHAPTER 2
# A Matter of Discipline

We're starting with a chapter dealing with discipline because we have both experienced times in our lives when self discipline has eluded us.

This chapter contains two stories, which together show distinct points on a continuum of abstinence versus indulgence. One story discusses over-eating, while the other deals with an addiction to smoking (although in both cases the subject matter is not so important). These stories are remarkable because both storytellers end up being comfortable at different places on the continuum. By making and fully owning their choices, they made it possible to reach their respective goals.

## Judy's story

Judy is in her middle years and describes herself as having a 'portfolio' life. She works as a business consultant, helps a friend who is developing a wedding business and practices a diverse range of home crafts. She has accepted that being a stone (six kilograms) overweight, but feeling in control, is good enough.

My first memory of loving sweet things is associated with my father, who adored Belgian chocolates. He would always bring them home from business trips for my mother, my brother and me. They were beautifully presented in gold boxes, tied with matching gold organza ribbon. They were really special and I loved them! The responsibility for developing my sweet tooth was also shared by my mother. She is a fabulous cook and would bake the most wonderful cakes, biscuits and scones, which we'd enjoy each day when we returned home from school. So my history of eating sweet things and good food was established at an early age!

I find that I've inherited some of my mother's traits and I, too, really love to cook. Being in my kitchen, trying out new recipes, making cakes, jams and chutneys and providing food for family and friends are all things I love to do. Even when I'm on my own, it's a real pleasure for me to sit down in the afternoon with a cup of tea and a slice of homemade cake. It's part of the joy of living. It is part of who I am.

I haven't always been this controlled, however. I remember a time in my career when I felt very stressed, because I had to confine myself to my office to do budgets, a task I absolutely abhorred! To prepare for this task, I'd pile my desk full of chocolate bars so that comfort was at hand. I was sure they'd help me through moments of tension as I tried to balance the books. And, in a strange way, munching those chocolate bars as I worked did sustain and support me during this fraught activity. The taste and the texture of the chocolate as it melted in my mouth would take me back into a world of indulgence, where I could escape the rows of bloody figures! Anything to numb me from the laborious task that I neither felt competent to perform, nor confident to get right.

As a result of this, I began to turn to food, particularly chocolate, to help me through all stressful situations – and there were many of them at work! On a good day, I would satisfy my needs with a piece of fresh fruit or low-fat yoghurt, but on a bad day I didn't want yoghurt, I wanted biscuits, chocolate and cake. And not just one biscuit, one piece of chocolate or one slice of cake – I wanted loads of them. I was on a roll!

In my attempt to control my eating, I attended a number of different weight-loss programmes and followed the established dietary wisdom. I monitored my daily intake of fats and calories, exercised when possible and weighed my body regularly. My early successes were followed by disappointments, and I entered a long period of yo-yo dieting where in time my losses and gains cancelled each other out. My life was dominated by food. I seemed to be thinking about little else.

The trouble was my reluctance to address the underlying issue, which was my unhappiness at work. Eventually, I became so unhappy that I decided to leave. Once I had taken the decision to change the course of my life, I found it easier to control my desire for comfort food. I made a lot of adjustments and decisions as a result, but of these changes, I decided that how I looked was not half as important as how I felt. In the aftermath of this experience, I no longer focus on the shape and size of my body. I am more concerned with the quality of my life and the people in it. I really felt, 'For God's sake, there are more important things in life!'

After this, I completely turned my attention away from how many calories I was eating and whether I could fit into my favourite old clothes. In fact, I threw the most menacing garments away, and instead of harbouring sadness that I couldn't fit into them, I came to terms with not being able to regain the figure I once had. I'm not the weight and shape that I used to be – I'm never going to be – but I'm going to live with that – happily.

The benefits to me are both surprising and dramatic. Now, I enjoy my food much more because I don't feel guilt at the pleasure I take from it. Instead, I exercise choice about what I eat and don't eat and I make my choices freely, day-by-day. If I'm having a good day, I'll reduce my calories and I'll feel happy eating very healthy food. When I'm tired or upset, I'll spend time in my kitchen and I'll bake a cake or home-made shortbread and enjoy the pleasure it brings. By taking my eye 'off the ball', so to speak, I find that 'the ball' is no longer a problem. I don't look at the cake and say, I shouldn't eat this cake. I look at the cake and ask myself: what do I need right now? If I need some comfort, I take a slice. No *should*; no *ought*; no *pressure*.

The re-evaluation I went through and my decision to accept a compromise was very important to me and has changed the emphasis of my life. The true answers to a few stark questions revealed to me what was really important and enabled me to make a decision to let go of a lot of unnecessary angst. Of course, I may not have been able to reach the same conclusion when I was younger. Different values and different pressures may have prevailed, but I'm pleased with this accommodation and I really enjoy the freedom it brings. I may still be about a stone overweight, but I see this as the price of my acceptance; and the peace that I have found is a price worth paying, in my view.

If I were offering someone the benefit of my experience, I would say, try to be truthful with yourself about what really matters to you in life and why. For instance, did I really need to be a size 10 to be loved or feel good about myself? Although the love of my family and my friends is most important to me, I know they don't love me for the size and shape that I am – because I've asked them! They love me for my other qualities, and it is these that I prefer to focus upon. This new-found freedom allows me to enjoy family gatherings, special occasions, friendships and my interests. I now use the energy that I used to spend on my anxieties on having fun.

I am relieved to say that I no longer obsess about my weight, and my husband is delighted about that! I accept that I have a few lumps and bumps here and there, but I can manage these with slightly looser clothing and different styles of dress. I must say, I'm very happy with my choice. This reality check has helped me maintain my weight within a particular range and I don't beat myself up if it fluctuates. I truly recommend it, especially at mid-life.

Judy reconsidered what was important to her after a life-changing appraisal. This resulted in her re-evaluating her priorities and enabled her to come to a place of compromise that has released her from the constant round of binge-eating and restraint. For Judy, it seems like a change in perspective held the key to managing her indulgences.

Our next story is about choosing not to smoke, and reaches the 'total abstinence' end of the continuum.

## Maya's story

Maya is a 27-year-old successful business consultant, who is just about to move to another position within a new organization. She lives in central London with her long-term boyfriend. She loves art, theatre and literature.

I was nine years old when I first tried smoking. My mother used to smoke about once a year, so there was a packet of cigarettes that had been in the house for ages. I'd heard people at school talking about how they were smoking, so I was inquisitive. Not thinking about the smell, I lit up in the bathroom. My mother thought that someone had broken into the house, so I had to admit to her that I had tried a cigarette. And it was horrible. It made my back go red all over and it made me cough. Years later, when I was in my early teens, my best friend and I spent a long time learning to smoke properly. I remember standing outside, practicing how to inhale. It was so exciting to have worked out how to do it. I didn't smoke habitually after that, though. It was more of a 'naughty' and exciting thing to do at the weekends, when I'd buy a packet and share it with my friends. It only became habitual when I was older and started to socialise with people who smoked regularly; I was about 17 and at college doing my 'A' levels. Also, I started a relationship with someone who was a smoker, so it became very much a part of my life.

When I hadn't had a cigarette for a while, I'd feel anxious and panicky, and I'd fixate on having a smoke. Smoking satisfied my needs until the feelings reappeared later. Then I'd have another cigarette. And so it went on. I was pretty free at this time and my life was under my own control, so I could more or less do what I wanted. There was almost never a situation when I wasn't able to smoke, even at work, so there was no real incentive to stop.

Finally, I noticed that my health had begun to deteriorate. I had a perpetual cough, which wasn't terrible, but it was there all the time. And I felt really lethargic. This was the worst thing. Every time I smoked a cigarette I felt completely drained. It was most obvious in the mornings. I'd get up feeling reasonably OK and get ready for work. Then I'd have a cup of tea and a cigarette. After this, I'd feel groggy and horrible and polluted.

As I got older, I knew that it was likely to be having a permanently damaging effect on my health. I guess the main thing was a realisation that it didn't feel like a choice any more. If I did carry on smoking, I'd have to accept the almost inevitable consequences of a life that was less fulfilling – smaller somehow – and probably, ending earlier. Also, I talked about the freedom to do what I wanted but actually, smoking was incredibly restrictive. It was a trap. I was constantly worried about when I was next going to have a cigarette.

I had toyed with the idea of stopping smoking for some time. (I was taught to use the word 'stopping' not 'giving up', because 'giving up' suggests doing without something that leaves you reduced in some way and, of course, stopping smoking is not reductive.) However, the day I decided to quit, something horrible happened, and the memory is still quite vivid.

It was probably about a month or so before I moved out of my flat to move in with my boyfriend. Usually, he stayed with me each night, but he wasn't there on this particular occasion. I don't think there was anything wrong between us; he just wasn't there, so I was completely on my own. I'd moved bedrooms temporarily, just prior to leaving, so I wasn't in a comfortable, familiar space. I just couldn't sleep and in the middle of the night, alone in the pitch black, I felt overwhelming fear about my smoking. In my fear, I felt I couldn't bear to have these feelings any more. I really felt as if I had reached my limit. When you're 10 years younger, you think you'll stop smoking by a certain future age, but at 27, I wondered how long I could go on saying this because I could develop cancer, or something, within another 10 years. I probably got up and had a cigarette because I was so scared, which is the whole irony of it, but there was something about that experience that really brought it home to me. I mean, feeling alone that night made me horribly aware that we all die on our own, don't we?

I think a big part of the decision-making process for me was not only the realization that I'd smoked for ages and might not get away with it for much longer, but also that I was getting older and I'd found a committed relationship. Now, it was not all about going out and having fun at the end of the day, but building a life for the future. I anticipated that I would need some form of support to enable me to succeed as I was committed to becoming a non-smoker – no cigarettes at all!

I found a method[1] that helped me stop wanting to smoke instead of putting me through the hell of using will power alone. This particular method holds that smoking is not a 'habit', but an 'addiction'. So, when you're anxious and tearing your hair out with the craving for a cigarette, it's nothing to do with the physical withdrawal of nicotine, it's all just in the head! Realizing that my smoking was 'an addiction', I was

[1] Allen Carr's Easyway to stop smoking: http://www.allencarrseasyway.co.uk/

able to follow the method and stop smoking.

Stopping smoking made me realize that I didn't give myself enough credit for being able to deal with difficult situations. I thought my ability to cope was all down to the cigarettes, but it wasn't. Today, I am able to cope without them, and now I deal with my emotional needs directly, head-on. For instance, if I'm feeling anxious or panicky, I don't pick up a cigarette; I pause, perhaps make a cup of tea, and try to work out what's going on.

I did have one or two false starts, it wasn't all plain sailing. I tried to give up a couple of times before. The first time using will power – that lasted about two weeks! And the second time unsuccessfully using the method that I've described above (I think I wasn't convinced!). I suppose I could have said, 'Oh sod it!' after these two attempts and just carried on smoking, but I had spent lots of time and money in trying to give up and I was determined to carry on. However, I'm very pleased that I've done it now. At the beginning, I had a real feeling of elation – a sort of freedom – and I just felt so incredibly grateful that it worked. Now, as time goes by, and I get further and further away from the memory, I just know that it's worked.

If I was talking to a smoker now, I would recommend getting proper support and help with giving up. In the approach I followed, it was important to step outside of myself and see my patterns objectively. I had to challenge all the subtle messages I found in magazines, advertising and films, and ignore the reinforcement that I got from other smokers. I also had to unravel the many contradictions inherent in smoking. For instance, as a child, you're told that it's bad for you, yet you see lots of people apparently enjoying smoking. It would be easy to conclude that there must be something good about it because otherwise, why would people do it? So, there are a lot of influences and assumptions to unravel in your head and you can only do this if you step back and see the different elements that make up your beliefs from a critical perspective. It's like a jigsaw – you have to have all the pieces to complete the picture and create a new mindset.

**Understanding Your Emotions**

As we heard these stories, we were interested in the varying degrees to which Judy and Maya were able to interpret and manage information from their emotions. After all, emotions pull our strings and push our buttons, making them great signals for appreciating that something is happening in us. Understanding our emotions is key to making informed, autonomous choices, because it puts us in the 'driving seat' of our own lives. It seems that the better we understand our emotions and are able to manage them, the more we will be able to make appropriate choices for ourselves.

Judy demonstrated that she had learned to interpret her emotions and use them to inform her choices. Maya met her emotions head on. She tried to understand what was driving them and chose how to respond to this. So, we propose that by learning to decipher the signals that our emotions send us, we can make choices about how we exercise discipline, rather than let our emotions run away with us and sabotage our discipline.

In hearing the stories and reflecting on our own experiences, it appears that the rhythms that surround good choices are wise and natural. Sometimes, if we feel uncertain, it may be that it's not the right time or place to make a decision. Judging the 'right' moment is a matter of instinct and intuition; we feel it is just as important to access and consider the 'unseen' information as it is to take account of what is more obvious to us. We have observed that if a choice is forced through pre-empting the natural process by which choices are made, we are more likely to encounter pitfalls. A forced choice could be a false choice.

We have already stated that this book is not about *what* choices should be made, but *how* you make them. We believe this because it is you, the reader, who has to feel comfortable with your choices and it is you who has to live with them. There may be lots of people out there with strong opinions about what you supposedly 'should' do, but they don't have to live with the consequences. We believe, therefore, that having the tools and the know-how to make good choices is a vital part of healthy living. If we can learn this art and take on the responsibility for practicing it honestly, we will surely have happier, healthier and more truthful lives.

The toolkit that we will be building throughout the book is designed to help you strike the balance between what needs to be done today and what you aspire to do tomorrow. If your aspirations are heartfelt and meaningful to you – and they belong to you – they will provide a context within which you can make good choices on a daily basis.

CHAPTER 3
# A Matter of Tomorrow

In our coaching work, we often encounter people who feel restless and wonder where they should go and what they should do with their lives in the long term. For this reason, we wanted to find a couple of stories from people who had made choices within the context of their long-term vision.

Our first story is from Angela, who made a life-changing choice as it became apparent that her dream of having a committed relationship and building a family could not be realised with the man she loved.

## Angela's story

Angela is 30 years old. She works for a prominent university as a clinical trials administrator. She lives in the heart of a university town, where she rents a room in a house with three other people who are either postgraduates or professionals. Angela has a younger sister who lives in London. She talks of the difficult choice she made when 'love was not enough'.

I recently decided to leave my fiancé. We had been living together for 18 months. We first met when we were both 15 years old, and we've been in an 'on-off' relationship ever since. He proposed to me on my 30th birthday. I couldn't have been more delighted. I felt great! It was also quite natural for us to be planning a future together as we were very much part of each other's lives and the lives of our families. However, it gradually became clear that our goals and aspirations were vastly different, despite agreeing in theory that we both wanted marriage and a family. I began to realize that this wasn't a good relationship for either of us. So, with tremendous sadness and pain, I made the decision to move out and pick up the threads of my own life.

After we became engaged, and once the new sparkle had disappeared, we seemed to set off down this very gentle, slippery slope. When he proposed, I was absolutely thrilled and completely committed to him; after all, I had wanted this for about 15 years! But then things started to go wrong, bit by bit, over the months. He was long-term unemployed and this led to money stresses, amongst other things. At the same time, I was beginning to find success. I was doing the best job I'd ever had. I was running a successful writing group and I was getting more involved in community events. I was feeling respected and valued for the first time in my professional life, having worked as a care worker for the previous 10 years.

Slowly, it became apparent that the more and more successful I became, the less and less successful he appeared. I think this difference in our situations was responsible for the first cracks in our relationship. These were prised open further by an uneven preparedness to do the household chores, a lack of money and a sense that we were each trying to survive on our own, not as a couple. I felt disrespected; he felt unsupported. I wanted things to be resolved; he was happy to 'let things be'. I wanted to be at the top of his list; he had other priorities. I liked to plan things; he liked to be spontaneous. I stayed with it for a long time because I thought we could work through our problems but after a while, I realised that I was getting more and more unhappy and less and less hopeful that we could be fulfilled together.

We had already had a conversation about me moving out, thinking that if we lived separately but close by the pressure would be off and we could get to know each other again; and I thought he'd realize how much he loved me and how scared he was of losing me! But I think I was just grasping at straws and trying to put off the inevitable, because at that time I was still committed to the marriage and was looking at any option to give us a chance. Moving 'out' but not 'on' seemed like a good idea. Leaving was too final; too frightening. When I did find a house to live in, it suddenly became what it was, a splitting up; an ending. I was terrified when I agreed to take the house that I'm living in now. The week before I left, we'd spent more time together than we had done for a long time, and it was lovely; so even at the point of departure, I felt there was a grey area. Will he let me go? Is there still a chance? Will he change? Will I change? Am I throwing away everything I ever dreamed of? Anyway, I did go. He didn't stop me. And here I am, feeling better each day.

Looking back, I can see that becoming 30 was a massive turning point – and the beginning of the end. Until that time, I was more or less happy to leave the planning (such as it was!) to my fiancé. But once 30, waiting didn't seem so attractive. When I was a child, I thought by this time I would be married, with a mortgage, and either have children or be planning to have them. As we descended our slippery slope, it became increasingly clear that these things were not going to happen. This realization was so stark that I felt I had to choose between my desire to have a home and family, and marrying my fiancé, who was apparently unable to provide this for me.

It was an incredibly hard decision. After a 15-year history, my fiancé was practically a part of my DNA.

But I was fortunate enough to have the support of my family, which freed me to not worry about money or the practical side of things. I knew that I wouldn't be alone if I made the decision to leave, and that gave me the freedom to see what choices were available to me. Before that, I had felt trapped.

In making my choice, it was almost like I was putting each option in the pan of a weighing scale: the prospect of getting married to someone I'd loved for years, versus the dream of building a stable home and having a family. Sadly, and somewhat bewilderingly, these two dreams were in separate pans. During the 'slippery slope' period, I could see the pointer moving away from the marriage. Suddenly, when I was 30, the pointer flipped. I had to make a choice.

This has been one of the hardest periods of my life and I've had to find courage I didn't know I had! In our relationship, I always 'bowed' to him and felt somewhat inferior. When I began to show concerns for the quality of our relationship, he suggested that I needed to get help sorting my head out; that *I* was the problem. He suggested too that I wasn't seeing 'reality', that I was not able to grasp something inherently concrete and obvious. I was aware of my own shortcomings within the relationship, but I felt that he couldn't see or accept his own contribution to the deteriorating situation. As I said before, we did try and fix it by talking a lot and putting little 'rules' in place, but our fundamental incompatibility became impossible to ignore. However, having made the decision, I now feel 'bigger'! I tell myself that I *am* an attractive, intelligent woman and that I *do* deserve better; and I'm beginning to believe it!

Of course, it wasn't as smooth as I've painted it. I've had my wobbly moments, when my feelings of love for him have come back and it has been tempting to think that this is the only important thing. So I'd be lying if I said there wasn't still a tiny bit of hope. But this tends to be outweighed by the moments of high tension. There were times when I became angry – very angry – and neurotic, and jealous and moody. As always, he received me calmly and coldly, which did nothing but add to my frustrations. We just weren't communicating. As I was leaving, he did panic and say, 'If you love me, you won't leave!' But what about him loving me? Another moment of clarity. I felt calm and in control. I walked away. I was sad, of course, because I felt he had created this situation, that it was all unnecessary really, and such a waste. But that was the way it was. That was 'reality', his favourite word! I do still love him. I think I always will. But each day, as I get into my stride, I feel more vital and fierce, ready to live to my potential and follow my dream. And, as I discover more about myself, I realize that I've made the right choice. And each day, as I wake, I make that choice again.

If I was offering someone a tip to help them through a situation like this, I'd say: don't lose yourself. I think it's important to try and get a new perspective, whether that means getting away or just having quiet time on your own. I think it's really important to challenge the logical voice in your head too, and listen for the quieter voice that is your gut instinct. Also, get support and validation from others you care for and who care for you. Tell yourself you are worth it! Can I just say one more thing? That you need to keep reaffirming and stay focused on what you want.

Angela described the 'stark realization' that even though she loved her fiancé, this was not enough to enable her to achieve her dream. She had a vision of what she wanted and she'd invested time and energy in bringing it to fruition. Then the moment came when she realized that it just wasn't feasible. The 'disconnect' between reality and her vision for the future created difficult feelings for Angela that forced a choice: 'Do I give up on my dream and accept, instead, something that might "do", or do I honour my dream and pursue it relentlessly?' Is compromise good enough?

For some, after examining the choice honestly, it may be enough, and so it becomes a conscious decision to choose to live with the existing situation. For Angela, she decided that her relationship fell far short of what she wanted; and even though it was very painful to leave the man she loved, she 'challenged the logical voice in her head and listened for the quieter voice that was her gut instinct.' When she did this, she knew she had to leave. After all, she told herself she was worth it. She was worth listening to and her dreams were worth honouring.

## Listen to Your 'Inner Voice'

When Angela started listening to her 'inner voice', it made her aware of the first cracks in the relationship. The more successful she became, the less successful her fiancé appeared. This is where Angela's personal courage and conviction was called upon and she had to hold on tight to her self-belief and all that it was telling her. It is hard enough for us to hear our own 'inner voice', but if our loved ones can't hear it, they can sabotage its gentle wisdom. Against the odds, therefore, we have to have the courage to give it credence.

We loved the notion of the 'weighing scale', as we felt this was a wonderfully graphic way of defining the crucial elements of Angela's choice. You may notice this notion of weighing up the pros and cons of choice in some of the other stories that are recounted in this book. Angela said: 'I could see the pointer moving away from the marriage. Suddenly, when I was 30, the pointer flipped'; then she said, 'I had to make a choice'. It seems that this image helped her find clarity and the courage to make her decision.

## Daisy's story

Our second storyteller, Daisy, describes her journey into higher education as a 'late bloomer'. Daisy is a 33-year-old mother of a two-year-old boy. She is married to a landscape architect. Daisy left school without accolade and worked in a variety of jobs before going to Australia for a year. Her story focuses on how she redressed the educational imbalance by attaining an MA in Ancient History as a mature student.

I went to a big comprehensive school with around 2000 students, and I got lost amongst them. The teachers always seemed to be telling me that I wasn't reaching my potential and my parents would get upset and frustrated because they knew I was intellectually capable, even though I wasn't delivering. When I did my GCSEs, in spite of doing almost no work, I managed to come out with some B and C grades. My father had been a lecturer and I think my parents really wanted me to go to university. I was the first-born child and you know what it is like: your parents, who think you're just amazing, only want to hear, 'Oh, isn't she clever?!'

I did go on to do 'A' levels, but I was just doing them because everyone around me was. I still didn't do any work! When I got my results, of course, I got three ungraded papers. My parents were obviously mortified. I think the reason for me not working was that I was so unhappy. I hated the school and I wasn't a very confident teenager. Also, I just didn't know why I was doing it. I wish somebody had told me that I could have gone out, got a job and earned some money! It would have saved me five years of having to re-take my 'A' levels (I got one grade E this time!) and failing to complete an HND [Higher National Diploma] in business studies.

The reason I left the course early was because the company that hosted my work placement offered me a job. For the first time, I felt welcomed and valued. The people were lovely and I really fitted in. We'd socialise a lot and they made me feel like I could do my job well. It was here that I realized my life wasn't just about academic achievement. After about two years, however, I started to feel a bit restless and decided to go to Australia to see some of the world. I was feeling confident and happy in myself and I suppose it showed, because that's when I met my future husband.

When I came back from Australia I needed to get a job to pay off some of the debts that I'd accumulated from my travels. I ended up in an awful job working on reception, filling up the hand soap and replacing the hand towels and free tampons! I thought, 'What am I doing?!' Then I got a job with a design agency and I became a project manager for them. I was there for just over a year and had to work really long hours. The values of the organization, however, were not mine and I began to feel stressed and unhappy. After a while, I knew I didn't want to be part of it any more but I didn't know what to do. I also didn't want this to be another reactive decision, so I spent a lot of time looking at job advertisements in the newspaper, wondering if I'd want to do the job that was being advertised. If I found one I liked, I'd cut it out and keep it in a file so that I could build a picture of what I'd prefer to be doing. Not only did this make me think that my lack of a degree was holding me back, but also I realized that I was seeking some form of personal achievement.

I seem to remember being in lots of social

situations where I was asked about my job and where I'd been to university. When I replied, 'I didn't go to university', I always felt like a 'lesser' person. I didn't decide to do a degree to make people like and admire me, but it did feel like an itch I needed to scratch. I thought: if I won the lottery tomorrow and money was no object, what would I do at this point? The answer came immediately: I'd go to university. Then I thought: why don't I do that? I also realized that if I'd gone to university as soon as I'd come back from Australia, I would have graduated by now; so if I'm going to do it, I may as well get started!

I started looking into how I could get to university and I found an access course, which involved two nights study a week for a year. I thought, I'll just see if I can get on it. So I applied and was offered a place. Then I thought, I'll just see how it goes! It came; it went. I finished with two grade ones along with my place at university, and by then it was as if I'd already started on my new path.

It happened so gradually and naturally that it was as if the decision had been made for me. I think pushing myself into a corner like this was a bit of a mind trick. I kept setting myself incremental challenges and then felt that I had to honour them or feel a failure! I wasn't really conscious of this process, but it was effective. That, and my husband encouraging me to stay focused on what I had to deal with and not to worry about what was coming round the corner. He would say, 'You've got to do this essay so get this essay done.' 'You've got to do this exam so get this exam done.' Then, I looked up and suddenly, I was saying, 'Oh my God, I've finished and I've passed!'

When I got my degree results I felt really, really flat. I thought it would make me feel different – like a better person – but it didn't, not immediately. When I graduated, though, it hit me and I was really quite emotional. I felt really proud of myself. Now, I have to remind myself what I achieved then. You can forget so quickly how much work you put in.

Did it change me? Perhaps, but it didn't change who I am. There was another thing happening when I finished my degree: I had a baby a few weeks after my final exams. I feel that I was deeply affected by these two events. The physical act of giving birth at home gave me a real sense of achievement. And the degree, in a way, was similar to giving birth. I had a similar feeling of, 'Wow! I did it!' When you're in labour and you reach that horrible bit where it hurts and it is really, really awful, you wonder why you ever thought it was a good idea!

At the very end of the degree course, I remember crying my eyes out in the toilet at the library when I was trying to finish my dissertation. I was in such a state! I could see people looking at me, but I was beyond caring. But from where I was sitting in the library, I could see the building where I would graduate and I just had to focus on that and think, 'You've just got to get this in!' I mean, my dissertation nearly killed me but, I thought, if I didn't hand it in I certainly wouldn't be getting a degree.

Then, after all the pain, the baby pops out or you get your degree, and you think: 'Wow! That's why I did it!' I'm still the same person, but these events have given me a belief in myself and in my capabilities that I didn't have before.

If I were to offer a tool or tip to someone else thinking about doing a degree, one of the things I'd say is find a supportive network of people who want you to succeed. And, whilst trying to focus on the task in hand, it is equally important to visualize why you're doing it – what's the end goal. I'd recommend visualizing what you're trying to achieve when you're in the middle of it all, or you may forget why you're working so hard and want to give up. These two tips sound as if they are opposite – big picture and little picture – but I think they go together.

The other thing I'd say is reaffirm your choice to yourself. When people ask you why you're doing it, it is helpful to have a statement you can use. Then, as you're saying it to other people, you start to believe it yourself and you become more confident in the choice you made. I used to say, 'I'd really want to work in a museum on the education side'. (Which is truly something I'd love to do.)

And finally, research. The internet can be quite confusing, but it can be a great resource; and whatever decision or choice you're thinking about making, just find out as much as you can about it.

Daisy is a good example of people who can identify what they don't want to do, but are not so able to articulate their dreams. In her account, she tried several different routes before being able to bring her vision into sharp focus. She tried 'A' levels and an HND to no avail, as well as jobs that were unrewarding and a spell travelling, before she settled on a concrete target. When we tried to isolate the motivation that enabled her to find her desired future, we found the 'quiet voice' of dissatisfaction that spoke to her (as she tried, and discarded, several options), and drove her to ask the big question: what do I want my life to look like? Listening to her 'quiet voice', Daisy was able to access her values, which were compromised and accentuated by her professional situation. Developing this ability to be sensitive to her own needs enabled her to visualize those jobs that she could imagine herself doing. Because of this, she was able to build a distinct picture. She was also able to acknowledge that her lack of a degree was holding her back and that she should seek a tangible form of personal achievement. If you see the possibilities for choice evident in what you don't want, it can inform what you do want. Eventually, this can reveal your life vision to you.

## Big Picture, Little Picture

Once Daisy had succeeded in acknowledging her desire for personal achievement, she had to meet the challenge of manifesting it, little by little, each day. This is where the 'little picture' fits in with the 'big picture'. Like a jigsaw puzzle – or perhaps, more accurately, a hologram – the tiny, sequential steps she made required her full attention and energy but then enabled her, slowly, to reveal the big picture.

Balancing the tension between the 'big picture' (future goals) and the 'little picture' (immediate activities) seems to be one of the secrets of making good choices. Too much 'tomorrow' and your feet can leave the ground. Too much 'today', and your long-term ambitions may be lost. Getting things done today, for tomorrow, suggests a clear route that can lead to success.

Daisy also said that if she'd gone to university when she came back from Australia, she would have graduated by now. This reflection kick-started her into action. This made us think about the phenomenon of 'time' and the way we choose to see it. After all, it is not like money, something you can accumulate, invest or save – it has its own momentum and continues to pass, relentlessly, whether or not you take action or wait. Therefore, why would you put anything off? You may as well act as soon as you can and get on with your life! Interestingly, Daisy found an immediate answer to what she really wanted to do by asking the question: 'If I won the lottery tomorrow and money was no object what would I do?' This seemed to release her from the practical constraints that she believed existed and allowed her to find a clear and instant answer.

Actually, as it turned out, Daisy qualified for assistance with the fees. Angela also said she 'felt fortunate enough to be freed from worry about money or the practical side of things'. This enabled her to see what choices were available. Before that, she had felt trapped and that her choices were limited. We were struck by the thought that, like time, how we chose to see money can impair or facilitate our ability to access the quiet inner voice. If a lack of money frightens us, we may be unable to see past this fear. After all, both Daisy and Angela's decisions didn't depend on a large sum of money. Both required some financial support, but ultimately, their success was not about that. It was about finding the courage and commitment in the phrase 'I can'.

# CHAPTER 4

# A Matter of Letting Go

People often talk about living in the present. To us, this means being able to bring ourselves fully to each moment and maximize the freedom to make spontaneous choices. It is not possible, we believe, to get the best from the present if you're preoccupied with the past. The injustices that have caused us pain can set up resentments that absorb a lot of emotional energy. Yet they do not have relevance after they have occurred. In fact, they just prevent us from getting on with what's facing us now.

## Mike's story

Mike works in one of Britain's leading academic institutions. He has responsibility for the infrastructure and the capital assets. He is married and lives in the country with his wife and a menagerie of animals. He is passionate about birds and loves to spend time playing golf.

> For about five years, I've been working really hard on the acquisition of a site for a world-class cancer facility. It was a difficult assignment that demanded commitment and perseverance, but it was one for which I had plenty of motivation because both my parents had died of cancer. The project culminated in a large ceremony, when the facility was opened by Queen Elizabeth. As a result of my involvement, I was looking forward to being part of the celebrations but due to lack of care and attention, my name was overlooked. Others, it seemed, who had not contributed as much as I, were amongst those invited. On questioning why I was not in the party, the response was dismissive as if to say: 'What's your problem?!'
>
> Although this was a long time ago, I still find myself harbouring resentment towards the person who was dismissive when I asked him about being omitted from the occasion. Although, no one knew the significance of this project to me, what I saw as his lack of recognition left me feeling dismissed and undervalued. When I think about what happened, those old feelings of rejection can return.
>
> If I were to recommend a tip to help people let go

of old resentments, I would say, conjure up an image, which helps you take 'virtual', but harmless, revenge. With a sneaky smile on my face, I conjure up the image of my perpetrator slipping on the banana skin that I drop surreptitiously as he passes by. Revenge is banana-shaped!

What's more, as a strategy, it may be worth telling yourself that you're worth more than allowing your energy to be sapped by holding a grudge. After all, who wins in that case?!

If we think about this story from Mike's perspective, we might appreciate the level of his commitment and contribution in reaching this important goal, which he believed was shared by others. In his mind, it would naturally follow that they would recognize and value his efforts in enabling the achievement of this goal. Knowing his huge contribution, he had certain expectations. Let's say we treat these expectations as his personal territory, which is surrounded by a perimeter, or invisible boundary, marking the extent of his values and beliefs. If we see it in this way, we might also see that his boundaries were disrespected or breached when he didn't get the gratitude he felt he deserved.

So, in our conversation, we felt that the issue of boundaries is really important in understanding the difficulty of letting go. Indeed, by knowing our boundaries, we are able to detect when they have been breached, recognize our response and make a choice about whether to react and how to do so. If we feel hurt or distressed, we may react quite defensively, for instance, and we may hold anger against the person who breached them. Perhaps this is because these boundaries are the layers of protection we create that enable us to face the world safely. Not only do our boundaries surround the territory that contains our values and beliefs but also, they hold our vulnerabilities and protect us when we venture into conflict or the unknown. Of course, these boundaries are unique and vary from person to person.

In Mike's situation, none of his colleagues knew that he'd had the sad experience of losing his parents to cancer. If they had known this, they may have been able to demonstrate the level of sensitivity that he needed. Understanding that everyone's personal territory is unique, we not only need to know and cater for our own boundaries, but also be curious about others' so that we can become more sensitive.

The following courageous story shows how, when our boundaries are invaded, we can develop patterns of behaviour, which can change the rest of our lives.

## James's story

James is a 46-year-old single man who has been through a lot. As a result, he is continually seeking self-understanding in pursuit of his full potential. He participates in personal development programmes with a group of like-minded people, which helps him explore his approach to life and the reasons for his choices.

James is working on a project to set up a self-sustaining development centre. He worked in the corporate world for 20 years and was successful in setting up a travel company, which was one of the fastest growing travel companies in the UK in its time. After recognizing that this was not fulfilling, he decided to leave the business world and pursue a path of personal discovery.

My story is centred on issues I had with my mother. She had many partners and I experienced her as someone who was unable to show me consistent affection. I remember feeling resentment against her when she colluded with my stepfather in his brutality towards me. But it was more complicated than this, because she brought me close when she felt threatened and needed love, and discarded me when she didn't. And, when my stepfather wasn't getting the affection he needed from my mother, he would take out his frustration and anger on me.

So, my resentment grew and I withdrew into my shell, turning from an outward, positive child to a confused child who spent a lot of time on his own. At the same time, I would try to get attention from them by purposefully being naughty. Sometimes, I would steal from our shop and bury things in the garden, knowing that I would be found out. Then I'd experience the terrifying footsteps on the stairs, which would be followed by physical punishment. But strangely, it made me feel as if someone was paying attention to me, especially as afterwards, my stepfather would show remorse with some glimmer of love mixed in.

Looking back, I could see that he and I were in similar places. We both wanted love from my mother, yet we had to compete for it. So, we entered this love/hate relationship, which was unpredictable but kind of united. We were even quite close at times, working together in the shop and talking about life in general. However, when I was 10, my stepfather's fury reached a climax and my mother took me and my sister to live with friends. I haven't seen him since.

This childhood experience left me quite confused and I pursued love in relationships that were edgy and unpredictable, but that I could manage and control through domination. This pattern repeated itself many times, with me sabotaging each relationship after a short while when the excitement wore off. Eventually, I found myself at the end of a holiday and at the end of another relationship, sobbing at the airport. I'd had enough of moving from one relationship to another and I couldn't stand it anymore. This was the catalyst for me to try to understand myself more, so I sought professional help.

Through this, I began to understand the pattern of my relationships. It started when I was about 17, after I had had my first intimate experience with a woman. Then I had string of girlfriends until I was 30, when I entered my first long-term relationship.

Before I was 30, I always felt the urge to keep looking out for the next person to fall in love with, perhaps someone with whom I could develop a deeper bond. I would fight very hard to get close to a woman, using my charm to entice her; but once I succeeded, I would find ways of sabotaging the relationship and bail out. The one thing I never did was cheat on any partner, though. I always stayed faithful until we broke it off. However, the energy I needed to meet someone new and form a bond was huge, and I began to tire of digging for this energy within me. Also, when I was in a single phase, I would look out for exciting, transitory encounters, to reassure myself that I was attractive, admired, and desired – and to boost to my ego. This was exhausting, too!

Through examining my behaviour patterns, I found that this was exactly what my mother had done to me. She drew me into her web when there was a drama and she needed comfort. I would feel her affection and be reassured and uplifted by it. Then, once she had no need of my emotional resources, she cast me aside and left me to fend for myself.

Interestingly, this pattern was also appearing in my professional life. I had decided that I would get everything I needed in life if I made myself a multi-millionaire. So I established a business that reached a £20m turnover in just a year-and-a-half. Yet, this too became boring, and at the same time as finishing my relationship, I left the business and focused fully on the personal work I needed to do.

Since that time, I have managed to let go of those old responses to my mother, and we now enjoy a much better relationship. Indeed, having detected a change in me, perhaps subconsciously, she is pleased to spend time with me and interacts differently with me.

Letting go, however, was tough because I had to acknowledge my patterns and the choices I had exercised to perpetuate them. I began to see them from a different perspective and recognize how entrenched I was in these patterns, unable to see the wood for the trees. It was a very uncomfortable place to be, but it was necessary for me to see my part so that I could move on.

Once I saw that I was a part of the pattern, and once I decided to change this, everything else changed, too. The world that was so familiar to me presented new choices that would either take me back to where I'd come from, or take me forward to a healthier place.

The good thing was that the part of me that used to collude with the established pattern also started to change, so a virtuous cycle developed that enabled me to feel more centred, secure and in control (exactly what I had, mistakenly, assumed I was before!). I must say, 'old habits die hard', and familiar patterns have their own form of comfort, so I experienced a bit of a tug-of-war for a while. However, the rewards for me personally began to be so great that the temptation to go back to my old ways soon disappeared.

Now, I can look at things differently and more dispassionately, which has increased my ability to 'let go'. I know my mother's history and the equal brutality of her childhood; I understand the reasons why she did what she did; and I believe she was not conscious of her choices – she was just doing the best that she could do. Her pattern was handed down from previous generations and once I understood that, and saw it for what it was, I was able to let my feelings of resentment dissipate. Being able to do this has been such a relief and the quality of my life has changed significantly as a result. I guess this is called 'forgiveness', and it is really liberating.

Not only that but also, in stepping back to take a look at my own patterns, I was able to see things in a 'holographic' way, which showed me their toxicity and the damage that perpetuating these patterns would cause me. If I wanted to free myself to form healthy relationships and enjoy life, I had to let go of this destructive behaviour. It took courage, but I now realise that I am responsible for creating my own reality and that I am in control of my own destiny. I would recommend this to anyone. I feel lighter, more stable and more confident than I have ever felt before. I believe it is everyone's destiny to be so released.

If I were to suggest a way of helping someone to 'let go', it would be to practice meditation. This has helped me a great deal over the past five years. I find it suits my temperament and is a really good way to start the day. It helps me to silence the constant chatter that prevents me from listening to myself. Once I'm in a meditative state, I can see how my mental habits control my thoughts and automatically send me into my old patterns. Of course, the mind is very complex and will pull you down many rabbit holes with trickery, but if you listen to yourself at a deeper level, you soon learn to observe yourself more objectively and develop greater self-understanding and self-control.

Through cleaning up and clearing out my mind, I have developed the ability to choose my responses to situations in a way I hadn't been able to before. I also find meditating is both peaceful and energizing, and I feel as if my world has expanded – that I'm part of something bigger. Meditation has given me new meaning and I think I would have gone mad if I hadn't found this tool!

In James's story, we see the power of making brave choices and the possibility to create new meanings and find freedom. Although you may not be facing such a situation yourself, it nevertheless underlines the value of understanding your boundaries and acknowledging the value of learning how to manage them.

## Recognizing Boundaries

We've already said that our values and beliefs mark our boundaries, but digging a bit further, we feel that these boundaries also hold the framework that brings meaning to our lives. This framework informs and directs our choices and actions.

By knowing our boundaries, we are able make decisions that we feel are 'right' for us. So, when we feel as if the boundaries have been breached, it's not surprising that it can be extremely unsettling and trigger some powerful responses, such as 'fight', 'flight' or 'freeze' – all of which are classic strategies for survival! We know, of course, that we all have our own set of boundaries and consequently, each of us is likely to respond to situations in different ways.

If we have a really strong sense of ourselves and our inner world is fashioned by the strength of our personality, then any 'invasion' from the outside can be dealt with from a position of confidence and our boundaries are preserved. Imagine feeling so certain about who you are that you are not vulnerable to others' opinions, words and deeds. Imagine you are able to invest in others while still maintaining your own integrity.

To be forgiving, we feel, it is necessary to be confident in who you are and what you stand for. In this case, you would be less likely to fear and blame others for their ability to hurt you, but instead take responsibility for your own emotions. From this position, there would be no 'holding on' and therefore, no need to 'let go'. To be such a person requires courage.

# CHAPTER 5

# A Matter of Acceptance

When interviewing people for this book, we often heard them say: 'I don't really feel as if I had a choice!' You will see from reading Roseanna's story that she challenged herself on this very point. Although Roseanna was dealt a 'bad hand' in the form of severe epilepsy from birth, she nevertheless found ways of making choices that have given meaning and joy to her life.

## Roseanna's story

Roseanna is approaching 50, a major milestone for many. She has an adolescent son who lives with her former husband, a short drive from the home she shares with her loving partner and carer. They live in a converted mill in Gloucestershire, amongst rolling hills and wonderful views. She is both an artist and an aspiring writer. She talked to us about her life, her experience of her condition and her choices.

I was diagnosed with epilepsy when I was nine years old. I'm now nearly 50. After the diagnosis was made, it was apparent that I'd had epilepsy all my life. Over the years, it has got progressively more intense, and as it gathers momentum, it seems that no treatment can control it. I have a range of different kinds of fits and they happen with no warning. This makes it very difficult to plan anything. I see it like a little 'being' trying to tell me, 'No you can't do that!' For instance, recently I was going to visit Highgrove Gardens with my friend, Annie, for her birthday, and I was quite looking forward to it. However, I had a seizure that morning and couldn't go. I was really sad about that, especially as I kept bumping into people that had gone who said it was lovely – and one doesn't often get the chance to go to Prince Charles' garden, does one?!

One of the trickiest times was when I was giving birth to my son, Sam. During the labour, I had seven grand mal attacks [clonic seizures]. Because of this, I don't remember much about the pain of the labour – a benefit perhaps! – but it meant that I wasn't safe to hold my baby afterwards. Although he was placed on my stomach for me to greet him, I had another major fit and someone had to catch him!

So, the epilepsy is a significant factor in my life. Wherever I go, whatever I do, I have to take it into account – as do those around me. Even making a cup of tea can be hazardous. I have often poured scolding water down my stomach instead of into the cup! And I have knocked myself unconscious, split my lip, broken my jaw and been badly bruised many times. The trouble is that I'm not really aware of what's happened straight after a seizure, so I carry on with what I was doing as if on automatic pilot, which can be quite dangerous if I'm injured.

Now, it is impossible for me to live on my own. I need constant observation and care. And I count my blessings that I have a wonderful, doting partner who does this for me. However, there have been some high costs for me to pay. Firstly, I have suffered two broken marriages. Secondly, I have been denied the pleasure of being a full-time mother to my son, who now lives with his father. He's a happy boy and he comes to visit me often. He loves me. He treats me gently, so I'm very lucky, as most adolescents don't treat their parents sensitively. But I didn't have the joy of bringing him up.

But you asked me to talk about my choices, and I do feel that I have them. I try to see the ridiculous side of my condition. It makes it easier to deal with. For instance, I've pulled down merchandise displays in shops, I've fallen through the arms of my partner, I've 'disappeared' mid-sentence and I've had to show my beautifully rounded – but burned – boobs to an extraordinarily hunky doctor!

I think I'm fortunate in having an upbeat nature, but I'm aware that I could become very unhappy if I didn't take control where possible. If I chose to focus on the danger, I would be frightened all the time, and if I chose to see the losses in my life, I would be depressed all the time. That's not how I want to live. So instead, I give my condition respect when I have to and slap it back if I feel like doing something rebellious, whilst taking the chance that it might rear its head again. I see it as taking back some of the power that has been taken from me; weighing up the options, thinking about the consequences, making a choice and taking a stand for myself. If I don't do this, I could end up being swallowed up by it.

If I find I can't, in all conscience, do something that I want to do because the risk is too high (like going to a wedding when I was suffering a bout of falls and risking stealing the show!), then, if it is too difficult for me to deal with the restriction, I'll curl up and go to sleep, or I'll make a point of finding myself something nice to do to keep my spirits up.

I guess I see my epilepsy as being like white-water rafting. I'm not going to swim against the tide because that's so exhausting. I'm not going to take extreme risks and beat the rapids, but I will coast with the flow of the water and find excitement in the speed from the safety of the raft. I also see it like trying to outwit my computer. If my computer is playing up, I love making it work how I want it to. I feel so pleased when I succeed in triumphing over whatever it is that is trying to make me do something.

I see myself as 'Roseanna with epilepsy', not an 'epileptic called Roseanna'. I am not stuck safely in a box marked 'epilepsy' that protects me from getting other knocks in life. I'm just as susceptible as others to loss, cancer and financial ruin. Of course, I do have my sad moments – I'm no different from anyone else in that respect – but I choose to be open to life. This is the joy of it for me: being open to every possible experience and seeing the lighter side of those experiences that may have unwanted consequences.

I believe it is important to make the best of what you do have and not focus on what you don't have. If I were to help someone find a way of accepting a situation that they did not choose, I would suggest looking at it from a different, perhaps humorous, perspective. I'd also say, balance your sacrifices with a reward, like an evening in with a good film and a close friend. It may help, too, if you see it as a game to pit your wits against. There are many ways to outwit an 'unacceptable' situation.

We were humbled by Roseanna's story. We both imagined that this condition would feel like a massive affliction. We could see how in the same situation we might feel overcome with frustration and fear, restricted by the ever-present potential for danger. The chance that we may have a seizure and hurt ourselves, shock and frighten others or become a burden and spoil a special occasion, would surely stop us from doing anything! It was very difficult to imagine a life where we were denied our ability to be spontaneous and carefree. We also considered how demotivated we would feel, having to deal with the impact of the shadow cast by epilepsy, obscuring any dreams we may have for the future. We imagined that we might feel that a large part of life was denied us and could hear ourselves saying the words, 'I can't!' over and over again. We thought we might look at others, apparently more fortunate than ourselves, and feel resentful that our life was limited by comparison.

Early on, Roseanna talked about the condition being extremely powerful in her life. Reflecting, but in an emotionally balanced way, she apportions her epilepsy with the failure of two marriages and having to give away the daily care of her son. She has huge – and from most people's perspective, justifiable – reasons to be angry at a condition that has cause her much heartache and sorrow, let alone the physical trauma. It would be perfectly understandable for Roseanna to be asking herself, 'Why me?' – an obvious question born of the all-consuming nature of her condition. But to our amazement, we don't see her asking this question, perhaps because she knows it is futile.

We saw the epilepsy as an intruder whose enormousness would overwhelm us and diminish our power. Roseanna referred to her condition as a 'guest', challenging her to make choices about the way she lives her life and the joy she can gain from it.

Roseanna also says that she puts herself in others' shoes and makes her choices while bearing in mind their likely reaction to any possible fall-out from her seizures. When talking to her, she cited examples such as being cautious around children in case a fall frightened them. She has also refrained from holding a friend's new baby, and she would stop herself from going too near a piece of valuable and fragile art. We found her concern for others showed enormous consideration and generosity.

What we notice about Roseanna's attitude is how she remains positive. She is always looking to balance the equation of really living her life on the one side, with the powerful, ever-constant presence of suffering an epileptic seizure on the other. She reframes her condition by saying: 'I'm not an epileptic called Roseanna, I'm Roseanna with epilepsy.' This is a really effective way of enabling herself to take charge of the situation and constantly transform possibilities into realities. These are all smart choices. Roseanna is so positive, claiming as much control as possible over the things she does in the most restrictive of circumstances and, as a result, getting as much as she can out of life.

By contrast, Mary's story may be less life-arresting, but she also grapples with an undeniable, inevitable situation, that is also beyond her control. This time, it is something that comes to us all!

### Mary's story

Mary is a professional woman who raised her son and daughter as a single mother. Juggling two full-time roles, however much she loved them, took their toll. As another year passed, Mary took some time out to visit her sister for some 'tea and sympathy'. This is what happened.

Recently, I had a significant birthday. I turned 40, which felt like I was over the hill. With the arrogance of youth, I have to admit: I never thought it would happen to me! Everyone was telling me that 40 was the 'new 30' and that life begins at 40! Sadly, I couldn't quite embrace the spirit of their message and this was starting to get to me. The beautifully backlit mirror that sat on the dressing table in the guest room at my sister's house reflected, perfectly, those unkind features that you read about in ladies' magazines. My skin was going south. My mouth was turning down. I had crows' feet on the side of my face! I looked closer and deeper in the mirror, wondering what I could do to outwit the ravages of time. My six-year-old niece, Emily, was at my elbow, looking up at me with curiosity as I pushed my skin against gravity and bemoaned the loss of my youth.

'What's wrong, Auntie Mary?' She asked, innocently.

'I'm getting SO old. What am I going to do?!'

Without drawing a sympathetic breath, she turned brightly on her heels and said, 'Live with it Aunty Mary!' And with that, she was gone!

I must say, 'from the mouths of babes!', and all that. It was a really rude awakening for me. That one so young could aim her words, and fire them so accurately to hit the mark, was amazing! And, it woke me up – to an extent. It was then that I started thinking about what I wanted to do before I *really was* past it. I had always had a part-time passion (is it possible to have a part-time passion?!) for ceramics. In the past, I'd had a wonderful ceramics teacher, who indulged my desire to produce pieces and facilitated my skill until I became quite adept at it. Alighting upon this, I soon began to fantasize about escaping the 'rat race' to live a more creative life. Well, I didn't quite go that far, but I did decide to enrol myself on a part-time ceramics degree – and that's what I'm doing now! So, thanks to my darling niece, I'm doing something I always loved, and doing it properly!

Although somewhat frivolous in comparison to Mary's story, it is true for many of us; aging can bring a degree of panic at the changes that occur and an accompanying loss of self-confidence. You may think it will never feel like that for you and then – surprise – it does!

The spectre of her approaching (although still distant) old age is clearly looming in Mary's imagination. Even though this process is unstoppable, there are still things we can do to take control, if Roseanna's philosophy is anything to go by; at least with regard to how we choose to feel about it. We may not all be comfortable with plastic surgery, but perhaps a fashion fix, losing a few pounds, a new moisturiser or hairdo might work. These choices may well slow 'the sands of time' and could help us feel better about ourselves.

But more importantly, we are brought back to the question of 'why me', which we're all prone to at times. Emily's comment, 'Live with it!' is really thought provoking. We see this as an invitation to take responsibility and choose to think differently about our dilemma. In doing so, it could open up a wonderful opportunity to change the quality of our lives. For instance, just like Mary, why not put your energies into moving on to something different, such as a passion in which you have not indulged for some time, or teaching yourself a new skill? In doing this, we are making good choices that give us back the feeling of control. At the same time, we may well expand our horizons.

From this we can conclude that when there seems to be no choice and we are faced with the inevitable, accepting a long term partnership with circumstances that can't be changed can give us the opportunity to stand back, see the options that do exist and get creative with our choices.

# CHAPTER 6

# A Matter of the Unexpected

This chapter focuses on stories from people who had the courage to make unexpected choices that were different from the majority viewpoint.

As you read Melanie's story, you may feel yourself supporting an obvious act of retaliation as a result of the extreme humiliation she suffered. Instead, she shows us her strength of character and her courage as she chooses an unexpected option, an option that delivers a far better result for her in the long term. Barbara, on the other hand, stood by her values in an extraordinarily distressing set of circumstances. At the tender age of 12 she showed amazing fortitude in sticking to principles she believed were right.

## Melanie's story

Melanie is a devoted mother who lives with her teenage daughter. She has an active social life and uses her business experience to run consulting projects on an independent basis.

> I met a man and feel deeply in love. I was so certain that he was *the* one that I chose to excuse the fierce independence he held on to and ignored the strange way our relationship played out over the next seven years. We both worked in the same company; we shared so much and yet so little. Plenty of work, plenty of play, plenty of talk – but no 'real' communication. Two people, two lives, two bank accounts – too different. I had needs – he did not do neediness. I wanted to make plans – he lived for today. I liked the idea of mutuality – he loved independence. I was fresh, young and excited by new experiences – he was emotionally scarred from previous relationships. His mother had deserted him. His once adored wife had an affair and left him. His brother and sister constantly disappointed and embarrassed him. Moreover, because of these experiences, he had a habit of leaving his girlfriends before they could leave him. I absolutely chose to ignore this history and in my youthful innocence held the belief that if he loved me, and I loved him, it would all work out. I would make changes and so would he!

The challenges that stemmed from his commitment phobia dominated our relationship and I couldn't work out how to articulate my needs or how to play the relating game with him. I didn't know what to do or when to do it. Yet I couldn't imagine a life without him. Then, I became scared – scared to stay; scared to go; scared at my own impotence; scared at my inability to choose. I wondered what had happened to me. Who was I? Yet from my wondering, something emerged. Was it determination, courage or desperation?

With the sudden onset of huge weariness accompanied by searing clarity, I realized our relationship was stagnant, paralysed, immobilised. I wrestled with my fears of loss and the changes that would inevitably occur. I also wrestled with the fear of loneliness, doubt, grief and isolation – and the shame of failure.

I didn't give in easily. First, I tried to talk to him. Nothing. Then I wrote to him – a very long letter explaining my fears, articulating my hopes and dreams and pleading for communication. Still nothing. He never acknowledged the letter. In the end, late one dark night, I said I was leaving, and I meant it. He said 'OK'! No more; no less. The choice was made, and whilst the leaving was pure hell, the time had come.

If only that had been the end of the story.

I returned to my single life, and threw myself into it with an energy and gusto I had not had for some time. In between the tears, heartache and pain of loss,

I laughed, smiled and joined in. This was mainly to prove to myself, and to him, that I was brave, able and independent.

Then on my birthday, he invited me out to dinner. And out of nowhere, he asked me to marry him! I was deliriously happy. Did I think I had won the jackpot? Did I think that by leaving, my 'plan' had worked? Did I think he had finally realized that he couldn't live without me? YES! YES! YES! to all those things!! Did I think he would change? Did I think we would live happily ever after? Did I think the issues that were there before would miraculously disappear? Did I think? No I didn't. I had no hesitation whatsoever in choosing to accept his proposal, and I didn't want to think about anything except how happy I was.

The wedding was slow to materialise. He had plans for a boys' week away; to appease his fear of the actual event, I suggested we got married just before that holiday, so that he could go away (on our honeymoon!) with his mates. And that's exactly what happened! We had a very small wedding in secret. Nobody knew. No family, very few friends and even fewer photographs. With hindsight it was not my wedding – it was a legal ceremony to make a marriage. I made it happen – he went along with it.

The next five years were happy, sad, miserable, contented, mad, crazy, busy, frivolous, and physically lacklustre. I truly loved and adored my husband but we were not physical with one another. We had lapsed into a relationship more like that of a deep friendship, and I felt empty inside. I was permanently tired and depressed.

I went to see a doctor in my place of work and explained my low libido. I knew the doctor. In fact, my husband and I socialised with her and her partner. This had some advantages, but it also made me feel very vulnerable. I chose her because I believed she would care enough to help and know what to do. I needed a swift intervention.

The next months and years were a blur of intimate consultations and counselling. I was finally (and very belatedly) diagnosed with severe clinical depression. My marriage was foundering and I was in bits. All through this, I was consulting the same doctor. Eventually, my husband and I agreed on a trial separation. There was huge grief and much protesting that we loved each other and would work it out.

I left my home and moved to a flat where, for several months, I examined my life. I considered what I had done, or failed to do, and what I wanted, even though I had no answer to that. I also reflected on the mistakes I had made and wondered how I might make things better. No answers came. I felt bereft and aimless.

I decided I needed to go home and work it out with my husband. After all, he said he loved me and love conquers all, doesn't it? I was unwell, but I believed that I could only get better with his support. He agreed to me going home, but he said he would not be there. For him, the marriage was over.

Immediately I jumped in the car and drove to our house. I collapsed in his arms begging him not to leave. I needed him to look after me. The phone rang and when he answered it, he pretended it was a wrong number. I remember feeling a very tiny click in my brain and thinking, who was that? I let it go. I couldn't cope – I was too terrified. My only desire was to keep him there, make him love me and make him realize how much I needed him. I cried. I sobbed. I pleaded with him to stay. He did stay that night, but in the morning he walked out of my life.

What I didn't know then was that he would never come back. There was also a lot more I didn't know. I found out that my husband and my doctor were in a relationship. This had been going on for some time. They had been found kissing in his office. They had even been away on holiday together. I had been betrayed, not only by my husband, but also by my doctor – both intimate and privileged relationships. So much treachery, so much disloyalty, so much subterfuge. So much infidelity, cheating, lying and manipulation. And worse, terrible professional and medical malpractice.

My first reaction was to lash out, hit and destroy her, and ruin her life as she had ruined mine. But I didn't have the resources to do anything. I fell apart. I cried. I went nowhere. I said nothing. I ate nothing. I did nothing except smoke, drink and sleep. I felt powerless, helpless and useless: a coward; a victim; a waste of space.

I existed in this state for a number of months until a time came when it just felt right to do something different. I chose tapestry, which I could pick up when I was feeling desperate, even in the middle of the night. I honestly can't, or won't, remember much about the sequence of events. However, the things that really helped me were time (a great healer), visits from my friends and family and, despite my earlier bad experience, other medical support. I also went through my photographs and cut out all the images of the doctor, which I burned. As a result of all of this, slowly I emerged from the emotional hell-hole I'd fallen into.

You may be asking why I didn't report the doctor to the General Medical Council for her lack of medical professionalism? I did not seek retribution because I felt I did not have the inner strength to withstand the inevitable scrutiny and ensuing emotional turmoil. I just could not face the process. However, in time I started to feel more capable and competent and I even made enquiries about how to instigate a case. But I calmly and rationally decided that my future was better served by leaving behind what I could and moving forward without further grief. As a result, I gained serenity, self-respect and some joy. Looking back, it was the right decision to leave it all behind and move on.

If I were advising someone facing the same situation, I'd say there really doesn't seem to be a shortcut through the grieving and suffering process when something cataclysmic happens in your life. The age-old saying that 'time is a great healer' was mostly true for me, but there were several important interventions, some by others and some of my own, which might be worth considering.

Once the crisis had passed, I tried to take each day at a time and be patient with my rate of progress. Every step forward, however small, had significance, and made me feel that maybe this journey would eventually end. I needed help and I received much support and care from friends and family.

I learned to ask for what I needed. I accepted medication and I believe that was helpful. The tablets did work, and I satisfied myself that they were purposeful and temporary. I took up activities that could be done to suit my somewhat haphazard waking/sleeping times – tapestry, reading and writing. I wrote everything down, especially at night when sleep eluded me. The process of defining in words the depths of my anguish was therapeutic.

I ventured out to 'safe' places where I wouldn't encounter thoughtless people who might try to invade my privacy. This was very important to me. Sometimes I wanted to talk, but only to those who genuinely cared about me, not those who wanted to 'enjoy a good gossip'. Eventually, I created a structure for my day-to-day life, starting with getting up in the morning and then returning gradually to 'normality', like eating at usual mealtimes, drinking less alcohol and taking more exercise.

I am a very organized person, and I used that skill to attack the chaos that I felt was around me. I tidied, threw things away, cleaned, washed and ironed; and these practical tasks were cathartic, as though I was cleansing my emotional dirty washing.

Melanie, despite justifiable vengeful feelings, decided to respect herself and choose a different path through her sense of injustice and pain. We felt that it took immense courage to shun the litigious approach, when the evidence was so clearly stacked in her favour. Yet it proved to be the right choice for her, the only person in the situation for whom she truly had responsibility.

Now we're going to turn to Barbara to hear how, as a 12 year old, she chose her own path, in spite of it being less usual.

## Barbara's story

Barbara runs a niche executive coaching business specializing in responsible leadership. She lives in leafy Hampshire with her husband and three children. At 40, she and her husband share the parenting and earning responsibilities.

The choice I'm going to describe is about why I decided to become a vegetarian, a decision that was very unexpected in my family and very much against the grain of everything that people around me were doing.

I grew up in Surrey, where my parents had a large plot of land. We moved there when I was aged three and my family set about tidying it up. We acquired various animals for varying amounts of time, including sheep (which we borrowed to eat the local bracken) and a pony to graze the grass. There were chickens (quite a few of them in fact), geese (three or four at a time) and sometimes turkeys. Because of this, I really understood poultry and the way they live and behave. The geese used to bite me from time to time, but I overcame that fear and managed to learn how to look after them. Not only did I become less scared of them but I also became more interested in them. Although we all looked after the animals, in the main, I focused on the hens.

At 12, I was very connected to the earth, the seasons and the animals. I would delight in sitting and listening to the hens making their gorgeous little grunts and noises. Just small things would really thrill me – I was very close to them. And the turkeys, I'd know their characters. I'd know which one was going to go up on the fence first. They used to sit there in a row, these huge great turkeys just sitting on the fence. I knew which ones followed and which one led.

The reason that this is important to understand is that we used to eat our own animals from time to time. Not regularly. Mostly, we took eggs from the geese and the hens, but from time to time one of our birds would make it onto the dining table. We'd eat Little Fat Fat or Curly Cross Beak (our nick-names for some of the animals) and I'd feel quite happy and comfortable because they'd had a long and happy life.

At about this time, I went to France on an exchange visit and stayed with a family we knew quite well. Although they could speak English, they never did, because they were trying to help me learn French. We started this particular trip in St Etienne. We drove for hours to Biarritz, where we were going to spend the rest of our holiday. Along the way, I had enjoyed the full range of French cuisine, including some of the country's famous delicacies. At one point, we stopped at a farm to buy some fresh meat. I didn't know it at the time but at this farm they were making *pâté de fois gras*. For this particular 'gastronomic delight', they were force-feeding the geese to make their livers as fat as possible.

Feeling tired after a long journey, I got out of the car and started to walk across the farmyard. Then suddenly, I stopped, rooted to the spot. I looked round this beautifully kept, pristine farmyard and noticed that the birds were absolutely the opposite. My immediate thought was that they were hideously ill. There was one particular duck, I remember, standing right in the middle of the farmyard with its wings outstretched trying to cool itself down. It was sweating. And I knew that birds didn't sweat – in the main, they pant to get cool.

My whole mind was focused on the question, 'What is going on here?' Then, 'How can these adults, who I trust, be allowing this to happen?' And, 'How could they not be flinching from concern for the birds?' Trying to work through that shock was simply dreadful. I could see that the animals were in distress. They needed help and, I thought: 'Who am I if I can't give them this help?'

Not only was the duck sweating and panting, but also it had lost most of its feathers. It looked utterly bedraggled and miserable. I said something like, 'Does the bird need a vet?' Which, of course, was met with much derision and laughter. And then they carried on about their business.

I could see the other animals were in the same state, yet nobody seemed to be caring for them or even worrying about them. I just didn't understand. There was a real disconnect between this well-kept farmyard and these birds that looked so ill. I was still standing there, wondering whether I could do something about it and if so, what I should be doing, when a man came over to a goose and shoved a funnel down its gullet. Bemused, I wondered, what on earth is he doing? Then he took out a cup of corn from the sack he was carrying and put it in the top of the funnel whilst still holding the goose, which was wriggling and trying to get away. Then there was some sort of corkscrew thing with a handle on it, which as he put the corn in, he turned. This forced the food down into the goose's stomach. And I just couldn't believe my eyes! I couldn't believe that I was witnessing something so totally horrid and no one around me was reacting at all. It seemed to be accepted. I didn't know what to do or say. I was just utterly, utterly shocked.

My host, realizing I was upset, told me: 'This is

how it's done!' They showed me the product in these confit jars and discussed with me what it was and how it was made. They made it clear to me that the process I'd seen with the goose was what made it possible to have this particular delicacy, and that it was renowned all over the world. It was, after all, one of the most French things you could possibly eat and one of the best indulgences after caviar! But they fundamentally misunderstood my quandary. It didn't matter what the farm produced. It was horrible. It was sickening. It was a disgusting way of treating another life and I couldn't believe that they were seeking to say that the outcome could justify how it was done. It just didn't marry up, in my view. We were just missing each other.

Because of my age and the language barrier, I don't think that the adults understood what I was saying. I realized they weren't seeing the same thing that I was seeing. For me, this was a completely new experience, and it really shocked me. There was something purposeful in that moment: who I was, my identity and sense of being became suddenly, clear... 'I am different from these people. I am not like anybody else around me. I have different reactions and this reaction is so strong that I can't ignore it'.

I was all over the place, feeling many different emotions all at once. I was scared of the farmer, actually, and I absolutely did not like the way he handled that goose! I felt that had I tried to intervene, I would have received similar treatment. I don't know if that was the case, but I was really scared. And I was angry. In fact, I was blisteringly angry, which was an unusual emotion for me. I was also sad, and distrustful. I was suddenly quite shaken, my sense of meaning and purpose all knocked about and jumbled up. I was very uncertain of everything because I was in a situation where I had trusted all these adults and they weren't who I thought they were. I had never, until that point, considered that I needed to know where my food had come from.

Afterwards, I remember staring out of the window of the car as we drove alongside the woods, which go on for miles on end in Les Landes. I was pretty miserable. Thinking back now, I attribute that to guilt and helplessness, but I'm not sure that I could have described my emotions very well on that day. Eventually I fell asleep. Then there was the excitement of arriving at the holiday house in Biarritz, opening it up, unpacking the *camionnette* (van) and deciding who was sleeping where. I remember pitching in to help carry things, happy enough to be helpful. I think, at this time, my experience at the farm had been pushed to the back of my mind.

That was until I was called to the table only to see a duck, beautifully served up, complete with head, bill and feet. It was adorned with lovely vegetables and it looked absolutely wonderful, but I just knew it was a duck from that same farm. Then with complete clarity, I realized that I was not helpless, that I had a choice; something inside me shouted, NO! I WON'T BE A PART OF THIS!

So I upped and left the table, which I have to say, is so unlike me, especially when I was a child. I was always ravenously hungry. I was an extreme 'foodie'. I LOVED my food. I was never knowingly underfed! And I certainly never left the table until any possibility of food was over. Everyone would think I'd have to be ill to leave the table! Shortly afterwards, my host came to see me in my room. I was sitting on the bed wondering if I was going to get scolded and told to come and eat. But I just explained that I couldn't eat that duck; that I thought that the animals had been ill and I didn't want to eat one of them. And, in my schoolgirl French, that's more or less all that I could say. At that stage, it was all they needed to know, but later in the week it became clear that I wasn't going to eat *any* meat.

I'm very much someone who wants to be loved, who likes to please others. But this decision, when I came back home to my family, was very much against the grain and perhaps seemed a bit critical of my family's lifestyle. I think that was why I was persuaded to eat a little meat from the butchers that had a 'free range' label on it. But my experience in France stayed with me, and when I understood that the meat industry got more money when they labeled a product 'free range', I began to distrust what was on the packaging, too! I also realized how much we are in other peoples' hands with food.

Although that moment in France was a 'big choice moment' – and I certainly forged my choice in the heat of that moment – I carried on making that choice again and again and again. For example, I remember people asking me: 'Are you not tempted by Pepperoni sausage?', or 'Don't you miss bacon?' – all sorts of things like that. Fundamentally, I didn't know where these foods had come from either, so I wasn't any more tempted than by ordinary cuts of meat.

Looking back on that moment, I think the language barrier probably helped me, because I couldn't descend into the nervous chatter that I might otherwise have done had my parents been there. Being just 12 years old and trying to speak in French, I could only muster simple language. So strangely, perhaps, I think I was helped by the fact that I had to search for the language and work out what I wanted to say. I actually went inward for answers, rather than outward. Because this was such an important moment, because I felt so deeply, I had to attend to it. I had to stop and spend some time listening to my feelings to make some sort of sense of it.

I don't want to be an extreme, fanatical or evangelical person, but I do want to be true to myself. I think this decision was quite different from others that I made in daily life. It taught me who I was. It taught me that what was going on inside is important. And it taught me what I was capable of.

If I were to offer some guidance to someone who was facing a similarly shocking situation, I'd say: take time away from other people to allow yourself to hear what is going on within. Remember what is really important to your identity, your sense of who you are, and how you want to be in the world. Make sure that your choices are true to that.

In our discussion of these stories, we wanted to highlight how these women created alternative choices for themselves. Although they had very different experiences, both Melanie and Barbara found themselves in totally unexpected and shocking situations, situations in which their firmly held beliefs about the world were shaken. What's more, these beliefs had not just been born out of dreams or childlike fancies; they were realities that had been confirmed by the words and actions of people who were close to them and in whom they placed great trust.

## Fractured Reality

Melanie's husband had confirmed her reality by telling her that he loved her. She believed, therefore, that by returning home, they would be able to work things out. Barbara had lived in close proximity to the birds her parents kept on their land and had watched them thrive through being treated with care and respect. Her reality was therefore reinforced by her observations and direct experience. So it's no wonder that when Melanie and Barbara saw and heard things which fractured their realities, their emotional response was extreme.

Barbara said, with amazement: 'I was witnessing something so abhorrent and others were not doing anything!' Melanie said of her doctor: 'My first reaction was to rush out, hit and destroy her, and ruin her life as she had ruined mine.' Both these statements convey a sense of being rocked and overwhelmed by emotion. And in the midst of this response, they were left without their usual intellectual resources – at least, momentarily. Having experienced a few similar moments ourselves, we could relate to the sudden disappearance of logical thinking when we are flooded with emotion. This is, perhaps, why Melanie and Barbara were left feeling overwhelmed, disorientated, upset and confused. Melanie talked of experiencing a 'meltdown'. Barbara remembered that she felt 'rooted to the spot'.

In these stories, we notice similar inclinations that follow this state. Both Melanie and Barbara disbelieved the reality that was confronting them. It was so extreme that it was outside their experience and expectations, and in both cases, it took them a while to gather and organize their thoughts.

Once the 'dust' had started to settle, they began to question the disconnection they had experienced between their outlook and others' outlooks. Through questioning, they tried to understand the values and motives of those responsible for the shock they'd experienced and find an explanation that made sense. But amidst the maelstrom of their emotions, no obvious answer was forthcoming. For this reason, they concluded that others saw the world as completely opposite to the way they did. People, we felt, cannot be expected to make good choices when in a state of extreme shock. They surely need time and space to work things out first.

As young as 12, Barbara was able to extricate herself from the dining room and distance herself from the source of her dilemma. Melanie, too, withdrew into her private space to give herself over to exhaustion and emotion. These responses seem to have been instinctive, and gave them the time they needed to get their heads around their shocking experiences. Considering this, it seems that when we suddenly find that our reality is not the same as others' reality, it is a signal for us to step back and examine the gap between the two. This probably sounds cold and calculated, especially as our natural inclination may be to rush in and try to re-establish the existing connections. However, instead of reacting impulsively, we may make better choices if we take time to let our emotions subside, so that we can begin to understand our feelings and try to work out what's happening to us.

## Taking Time

Strangely, the thing that seemed to help both Melanie and Barbara was their lack of preparedness for the situation they faced. Melanie retreated in exhaustion: 'I cried. I went nowhere.' Barbara said: 'The fact that I didn't understand the language, cut out the chitter-chatter in my head.' In their disbelief, and in their inability to make any sense of the situations they found themselves in, they nevertheless were able to access resources inside themselves that they hadn't known were there. And, having had these experiences, they now have the 'language' that will help them deal with similarly bewildering situations in the future.

The pressure on Barbara to 'follow the crowd' and view the practice of producing *pâté de fois gras* as acceptable was enormous, especially when she saw adults as authority figures. As a 12 year old in a foreign land, she could easily have felt pressured to conform to the popular view. This would have been an understandable automatic choice. Melanie's understandable response, when told that her husband had been having an affair with her doctor, would have been to go after 'her' and 'ruin her life as she had ruined mine.' Instead of doing this, both Barbara and Melanie withdrew sufficiently to gain a different perspective. This enabled them to make the choice that, ultimately, felt absolutely right for them. The 'rightness' of her choice is underlined by Melanie's statement, 'It was the right decision to leave it all behind and move on', and Barbara's statement, 'I just couldn't be part of this'.

Generally, it seems we seek instant resolutions to shocking situations. Perhaps it is better to see 'time' as a more effective companion, instead.

# CHAPTER 7

# A Matter of Perspective

In the introduction to this book, we drew attention to the frequency with which people make a choice and then worry about whether or not they have made the right one. In this chapter, we are presenting two aspects of this dilemma from two different generations. We want to examine whether or not, as we get older, the way we reflect on our choices changes.

## Georgina's story

Georgina is a mature woman who was a child during the World War II. She has three grown-up daughters and three grandchildren. She has always been a colourful and distinctive character, with many interests. She is fascinated by philosophy, both modern and ancient, and enjoys exploring the landscape and local legends around her home in Somerset.

This is a story that describes a complex decision, which was made at a time when societal pressures and personal desires sat in opposition to each other. The detail, we feel, is important. This is her story:

I'm just coming up to 82 years old. I trained as a speech therapist when I was young. It was a new profession that was developed just after the war. At that time, it was absolutely untried and the field was wide open. I thought it was marvellous because we could collaborate with nearly 30 different professions. We interacted with, for example, top plastic surgeons, head teachers, social workers and psychiatrists, and I thought it was a fascinating job.

My husband was in the Army and we started building a family, with our first two girls born in the UK. When they were quite young, we were posted to Germany, where I gave birth to my third daughter. Just after she was born, the Chief Medical Officer (CMO) for the whole of the European-based British Army came to me and said: 'Would you come back to work for us?' At first, I said, 'No. My baby's new born and I must stay at home to look after her.' This was very much the convention at the time, especially in the Army, where officers' wives supported their husbands by conforming to the 'way things are done around here'. This really meant being a 'domestic goddess' and respecting the social hierarchies amongst the officers' wives. However, the CMO was not dissuaded, and went on to emphasise the needs of the clinical services and underlined their lack of expertise in my professional area. He said that I knew more than any of the doctors – including himself – because I'd specialized in subjects like neurology, psychiatry and social services as a speech therapist. And he added that they really needed someone who could judge if soldiers, who were stammering badly for instance, were too stressed and needed to be sent back home to England. Also, if a family had a baby who turned out to be disabled in some way, whether he or she needed specialist treatment in England or could be treated locally, and so on. So, I did agree to work for them.

My mother-in-law knew the parents of a pre-university girl who wanted to take a year out, so she was dispatched to work with us as an au pair, and the Army provided a driver for me. (Apparently, he had a skull tattooed in his armpit because he'd been a member of the SS during the war. He was rather sinister looking, actually!) Anyway, I could pretty well choose the hours I worked. So, while my older children were at school, I could tour around the different clinics whilst the baby was being looked after.

At that time, I was the only service wife amongst all of the troops in Germany who was working, so people had an opinion about it. Funnily enough, it was mostly the men who said things like, 'I couldn't afford to have help for my wife!' or 'My wife likes to look after the children!' and such similar things. It was not very unpleasant but I was aware that I was a bit of an oddity. On the other hand, the medical team was grateful for what I was doing and the support from the medical centres was marvellous, so it all balanced out. Besides which, my work made me feel fulfilled and useful. It was full of human interest and I felt I was really contributing to people's well-being and self-esteem. Not only this, but also I felt that I was contributing to my family and to society as a whole.

Thinking about my choices from here, I think I decided to return to work to compensate for the part of me that was pushed aside when I first made my career choice. When asked at school what I wanted to go on to do, I said I wanted to study art. It was at the time when people like Henry Moore were becoming known and great artists were coming together to rebuild Coventry Cathedral and places like that. It was so exciting. These places were like museums of modern art and I really wanted to be part of that world.

However, the immediate – and rather fierce – challenge from my mother was: 'And are you convinced you can be a first-rate artist?!'

At the age of 16, having been shown paintings by Michelangelo and having had the virtue of humility pummeled into me, I could only say, 'No. I suppose not. But I do want to learn.'

Then came the swift retort: 'Do you want to spend the rest of your life starving in a garret?!'

'Well, no.' I said, 'Not really!'

Two sentences and the door was closed! I don't suppose it was ever intended to be as final as I thought, but my mother was incredibly dramatic and emphatic. At the same time, I'd had about seven years of brainwashing in an unbelievably repressive Anglo-Catholic boarding school.

Then came the next question, 'So what would you like to be?'

I had recently reduced a rather well known actor to tears in a school play and he was convinced I should go on the stage and eventually into films. 'An actress!' I replied confidently.

My father and mother both reacted. 'You would be nothing better than a guttersnipe!' No argument there then! 'So what ARE you going to do?'

Searching around in my head, I remembered that one of the older girls who was, like me, a Gold medalist in Speech and Drama, was going to be a speech therapist, so that's what I said I would do. I wouldn't have even heard of speech therapy if it hadn't been for her, and I didn't know what it involved, but my parents relaxed and said that that was settled then! They were happy that I would be able to support myself, and reassured me that I could always do painting and acting as hobbies. Actually it turned out to be a really interesting profession and I always enjoyed my work. It was very varied, and I met some extraordinarily gifted people in many allied professions, so it was probably a good choice, in the end.

My mother lived by the maxim, 'If you are going to do something, do it with a good grace, or don't do it at all!' And I really did try to live that way. So, I suppose I simply didn't question this choice or feel aggrieved about being sent down a different path.

Many years later, when I was retired, I went to university to study art. That was heaven! And actually, if I were to guide somebody who was making this kind of career choice, I would suggest that they really examine their values and put them into the decision-making equation.

For me, my choice to work as a speech therapist after the birth of my third child made me feel that I was contributing to peoples' peace of mind and happiness. I felt I was helping to repair their self-esteem, and so had a good reason to be working. My schooling was extremely religious, and the whole thrust of the education was to learn to become a missionary, so with 'missionary zeal' I felt that I had to be of service to humanity. This meant that I set aside my first love, which was art and the life that was connected to it. Actually, because my schooling had shaped my values, I may have felt I was being self-indulgent if I had done art. I was trying to justify my place in the world – but perhaps I did this at the cost of being true to myself.

To put this in context, after the war, we had this huge upsurge of really inspiring women's stories. There were women engineers who designed, built and repaired aircraft, bridges and factories. There were women in the medical and emergency professions working as doctors, ambulance drivers and hospital administrators. There were women in the legal professions working as lawyers. There were women working on the land, and so it went on. The extraordinary thing is, just after the war, many of these women appeared happy to relinquish their important professional roles and return to domesticity, and they did so without any apparent resentment. Although this was a time of austerity (we were still being rationed and life was difficult), this was not something the women in my family understood. My mother was from a pioneering family that had lived in New Zealand. She lived a life that was unbelievably tough with her 10 siblings. There was no medial support, no power and no water or sanitary facilities. When my mother cut herself, her mother sewed her up with a darning needle and some strong linen thread, because there wasn't a doctor for hundreds of miles!

These examples of strong women were not lost on me and I felt compelled to rise to the occasion. This definitely put me out of step with those who set themselves aside and returned to domesticity to support their men folk. However, I was also out of step with my true, more creative self, as I didn't follow my dream of becoming an artist. However, even though I was living by acquired values at that time, I'm glad I did it because I felt better about myself, although I sort of betrayed my true nature; these days, perhaps, people might see that as wrong. I think now: I wish I had made more honest choices, but in fact it turned out to be a really good life and stood me in good stead.

As we listened to Georgina's story, we could really feel the dilemma she faced, which seemed to be pulling her in three different directions. She was concerned to serve society through her profession, yet had to go against the social norms of the time to do so. She felt the pull of her young family and had to withstand the criticism of not caring for them personally. At the same time, she wanted to pursue her passion for art, which she denied by using reasons that were influenced by her parents. Whichever choice she made, there would be two other important possibilities left unsatisfied. Damned if you do, damned if you don't!

Georgina made a controversial decision to return to work at a time when others' were staying at home. In this instance, she was persuaded by someone who inadvertently tapped into her values, which made it easier for her to choose. Her education at an Anglo-Catholic school also made her feel she HAD to do something to help humanity.

## Push and Pull Choices

It seems that when we make life-altering choices, many different influences come into play: some are external, as in the case of Georgina's parents; some are internal, such as Georgina's values. We wondered if there is a qualitative difference between these two types of choices and whether Georgina felt freer in making her choice when her values were blocked, as opposed to the choice she made from pragmatism and common sense? We thought of these different dynamics as 'push', when her parents intervened, and 'pull' when she was enticed to make the choice through her own values. We're not suggesting that 'push' and 'pull' are imposed types of choices; rather, they reflect the conditions that surround choice-making. The 'push' choice is when someone says you 'ought' or 'should' do something and you feel pressure to do so. A 'pull' choice is when someone says something compelling that helps you connect to, and access, what you feel inside, and enables you to make a 'right' choice for you. In Georgina's case, she was 'pushed' into making a decision through the persistence of the Chief Medical Officer, but in exerting this pressure, he also tapped into what she called her 'acquired' values, which 'pulled' her into the decision. Asked later how she saw this dynamic, she said:

> For me, when I was asked to work for the services, I suppose it linked back in my mind to 'supporting our brave boys' as the women did during the war. I think I was in a sort of 'Dad's Army' frame of mind, where one just got on with whatever was on one's plate and didn't fuss. And I lived in the moment as much as possible – more behavioural residue from the war. I was determined not to do anything that would reflect badly on my husband's career so, when I was not working, I supported him in pursuing his interests – he

loved sailing and amateur dramatics so I got involved in these activities as much as possible. Also, when I was working, it was a way of affording those extra things that had not been within our budget beforehand. But those are all rational arguments: the other thing I felt was freedom – freedom to choose in a way that I hadn't experienced before. Being in Germany at that time felt like being on perpetual holiday. There were lots of lavish parties and all the entertainment was laid on. It was the beginning of the 1960s and I loved the creative explosion and the accent on women as 'players' in society. That was marvellous. So, there was undoubtedly something in it for me. I felt valued and valuable, and I was having fun!

Even though Georgina carried and expressed her 'acquired' values, she acknowledged that they were not of her own 'true being'. Her 'true being' was creative, and as a result of having compromised her values for too long, she ended up feeling that she'd betrayed her nature. Yet, she fully embraced the notion of serving humanity; so even though acquired, her values nonetheless served her decision making for the rest of her life. We felt that if we compromise our values out of necessity (which we sometimes have to do), we could make better long-term decisions if we ask ourselves: 'Am I aligned with my values?'

It's interesting to note that Georgina's love of art never left her. It remained with her throughout her life, and when she retired, she finally had the opportunity to pursue her passion. This is a classic example of really listening to yourself at a young age, knowing yourself well and following your natural inclinations. Although in Georgina's case it was not possible for her to do this until later in life, we guess that this is not uncommon. We both agreed that throughout our lives we could have stayed closer to the things we loved, which may have resulted in a different approach to our choices and caused us to take different directions.

Even though we can understand the reasons for Georgina being persuaded to return to work (she was needed for her skills and expertise in a context that resonated with her formative influences), she still had doubts about her decision. She had to go against the accepted 'norm'. But this served her sense of purpose, contributing to people's well-being and self-esteem. The job enabled her to find a real sense of worth and identity. Georgina was able to justify her place in the world in the context of inspiring women. So, even though she didn't 'indulge' herself as an artist or an actress, she still found work with purpose and meaning, which enabled her to establish her identity.

Historical perspective is a marvellous thing, and Georgina probably didn't see herself being at the leading edge of a social revolution. However, the post-war period did herald huge change for women; reading Georgina's story, we thought it conveyed the sense that she had one foot in the more conventional camp and the other in the emancipated camp. Her choices seem to have sprung from trying to reconcile these different social dynamics – made more complicated by the influences of her childhood – whilst meeting her own needs for self-esteem and fulfilment.

### Sarah's story

Our next story has been written by Sarah, who at 19, is from a completely different generation. At the time of writing, she had just completed her GCSE A levels. She lives with her parents, brother and sister in the Home Counties and both sets of grandparents live close by. She has always loved music, reading and more recently, Lindy Hop. She has always found her schoolwork relatively easy, being blessed with a good mind. When she had finished writing this piece, she departed for Ecuador to do some voluntary work with children. She was due to be away for several months.

Before I start, I feel I should inform you that I don't make decisions easily. In fact, I tend to avoid decisions like the plague. They stress me out and give me spots. I have always maintained that the best way to handle decision making was simply not to make them – after which I reached a point where decisions were no longer avoidable.

I had sidestepped the one about going to university with considerable ease; I deferred a year so that the actual choice could be made later – so far into the future it was easy to forget about it for the time being. I had always known what I would study, languages being far and away my forte for as long as I could remember. The university options came courtesy of *The Times University Guide*, combined with which courses offered the best freebies at the convention we were all forced to attend as lower sixth formers.

Irresponsible I know, but I felt it was the most stress-free way to deal with something that was causing my friends all sorts of grief.

My problems arrived after the A level exams, which again, I took in my stride and didn't lose any considerable amount of sleep over. They came as the summer arrived and my friends exchanged their troubles for sunshine and picnics and all kinds of summery frolics. I realized that the decision to avoid making a decision had ironically thrown me into a much deeper pool than I had bargained for. I had a year to do whatever I wanted. I had time on my hands that I didn't owe to anyone but myself. In short, I had freedom that I wasn't quite sure what to do with.

I had always known that I wanted to travel. I wanted to use my languages, become part of a new community, and learn how to live outside my comfort zone. I wanted to leave England and try something different. I had always understood that in order to do this, a lot of things would have to be left behind. However, I had never quite realized how much I would care about the things I left.

I can see how this statement may seem slightly odd – that I knew I'd be leaving things behind, but I didn't think it would matter. Let me explain: I had always been a busy bee, one that spent most of her life trying to fit another activity into her schedule, and as a result I never really gave anything enough time to really care about it. Of course, hindsight is always 20:20 – back then, I just enjoyed the variety. I never stopped to think why I hardly ever saw friends out of school, or enjoyed a whole evening in front of the TV, or even got the kind of morning lie-ins that teenagers are renowned for.

It took until I was 17 to find something I wanted to make time for – that was when I fell in love with Lindy Hop, a swing dance from way back when ladies wore swirly dresses, ankle socks and victory rolls when they dressed up for a big night out. I started dancing two, even three times a week; I became part of a performance group, danced socially, and even started teaching classes after a while. I embraced it wholeheartedly, made it my life. My catchphrase really was: 'Sorry, I can't – I'm going dancing....'

Then he came back into the picture.

I'd met him when I started work at 16, and fell for him almost straightaway – my first experience of complete, mind-numbing stupidity in someone's presence. He was three years older than me, a first year student at university, with a wicked sense of humour and bright blue eyes with long eyelashes that smiled at me. Of course, it came to nothing: he left the cafe where we worked, I filled the gaps he left with other things, and we went our separate ways. Then all of a sudden, half way through my last year of school, I found him again. By the time my exams were over, we were together – an actual couple. It was amazing, more than I could ever have hoped for – I had found someone that I wanted to make the time to be with and who wanted to be with me.

So that was how making my first real decision became the hardest thing I'd ever had to do. I still had my little cafe job. I finally had my boy. And when I wasn't here or there, I danced and danced and danced, revelling in the freedom and the happiness that it brings. Life was as close to perfect as I had ever hoped it would be. Except for one little thing – my dreams of travel and excitement never quite went away.

It wasn't that I wasn't happy with my life – that's not true. But at the same time, I was bored of my job and frustrated with my family, who were constantly pushing me to do what I had always said I wanted to do. I knew I had to leave, find my independence and satisfy my curiosity about what lay abroad, but at the same time I didn't want to. As much as life at home aggravated me, I couldn't face the thought of not being able to dance. Even more painful than that was the thought of leaving him, after what felt like a length of time together that barely did us justice. I imagine there will be some rolling of eyes at a statement like that coming from an 18 year old, but just think: by that time I had known him for nearly three years. I had wanted him for all of those years. Yes, maybe I seem melodramatic, but to me it seemed reasonable. In fact, it still does.

I honestly didn't know what to do. So me being me, I kept putting the decision off, hoping that if I did nothing it might go away. It didn't.

It took a lot of painful nights and too many tears to

make the decision to go. In the end I told myself to be practical, reasoning that if I did go to university, then living alone for a year abroad, using my languages and learning to be independent would stand me in good stead. I would get away from my family, find a new job and have a break from the familiar. Of course I would miss him, but he assured me he would still be there when I got back. Since I wanted to believe him more than anything else in the world, I did – and I left.

In my new life abroad, I found a new job and new friends, somewhere to live, and the best place to do my supermarket shopping. I settled down and I managed. That's the best way to describe the first couple of months – I managed. It hurt every day not to wake up in a familiar bed, not to dance, not to see my family. Most of all, it hurt not to be with him – not to be close enough for him to wrap his arms around me every time I hurt. It got easier with time, and most of the pain went away as I became more comfortable with my surroundings; but when the time came to return home, I was packed three days early.

I won't say I should never have gone, because that's not true. As a result of my time away, I am closer to my mum than I ever was before – I am more open with her and she trusts me a lot more. I have more confidence to speak my mind. I know how to fix problems, and I know a lot more about different types of people. There is no doubt that I have gained confidence by striking out on my own. I've learned to appreciate the values of having family close by, and of good communication. Those are the good parts.

However, I have also become less proficient at dancing. My feet are lazy, not quite so sure of what to do, when they used to move like lightening. I no longer have the money to run a car, so I have lost the freedom that I used to have. For various reasons, the relationship I waited so long for suffered along the way – and although we are trying to rebuild what we had, it is a slow and sometimes heart-splittingly painful process as we regain the trust in each other that we once took for granted.

The worst part is that I'm not nearly finished – as I write this, I am planning to go away again. Not for as long, but it needs to be done, to fulfil the promise I made to myself at the beginning. Some people may see this as an opportunity to right a wrong, as it were; a second chance at a bad decision, the chance now to make the right one, to stay and carry on my life here instead of once again flying off to pastures new. The truth is that even if I can't give myself a definitive answer as to whether my decision to leave was right or wrong, I learnt things about myself whilst I was away on my own that will stay with me for the rest of my life; and I did things, good and bad, that shaped who I am today.

Even if I do sometimes look at what I lost and wonder if I would have been better off letting my heart rule my head, I would never discourage someone from going and doing what I did. I suppose that in most things you have to remember that there are negatives to every decision you make – whether you cut your hair short or leave it long, whether you go on that holiday or save the money, whether you leave your familiar life or stay and nurture it into something worthwhile. With this in mind I believe you shouldn't make decisions under the impression that each one could make or break you. Of course, some decisions are more difficult than others, but at the end of the day, any course you follow will have its highs and lows, and there's no point in tearing yourself up when you think you've got it wrong.

I think that the best you can ask of yourself is to handle whatever comes your way by looking for the positives – those things that make the bad bits more bearable, whether it's the friends you would never have found, the jokes you would never have heard, the food you would never have tasted, or the experiences you would never have had, and never have been able to add to the story of your life.

The silver linings are invariably there, waiting to be found.

Sarah's story is being related at a time in her life that is not so very different to when Georgina was making her choices. The difference between them is purely a matter of perspective. Georgina is able to reflect on the long-term consequences of her decisions retrospectively. Sarah is unable to do this. For her, the long-term consequences are as yet unknown. We might well wish for the power of hindsight when making life-changing choices!

The position Sarah finds herself in is a notoriously difficult one. Not only does she have to pass exams, but also the pressure on her to make the 'right' choices is immense. Newly out of the disciplines and constraints of school, where the day is dictated and the activities are prescribed, Sarah has to shape her own life. And, as in Georgina's case, the choices she makes are not small; they will have a far-reaching impact on an uncertain future where there are no guarantees. It is no wonder that the 'gap year' has become a popular way for students to decompress and think about their next steps. (In Georgina's time, of course, the gap year did not exist, so she could not take this option.)

If we don't like making choices, we often postpone or push them far enough away from ourselves that we don't feel as if we have to make them. Indeed, we may hope that they'll go away altogether! Sarah said: 'I realize that the decision to avoid making a decision had ironically thrown me in to a much deeper pool than I'd bargained for.' Hmm... How interesting is that?! It shows that a timely choice or decision can save a whole lot of angst.

It also true that it is difficult to know how you are going to feel as the anticipated time of choosing draws near. Sometimes, we are able to work things out in advance, but when it comes to the crunch, the reality can feel quite different. Having made the choice, Sarah makes reference to something that often happens, especially if we let our head overrule our heart. In her case, she withstood the fact that 'it hurt every day' whilst she settled into her new life. So even if you believe you've made the right decision, you may not be flooded with certainty and you may be called, time and again, to re-assert the choice that was so painful to make in the first place. But we also see that it gets easier with time. In this rocky place of doubt, we should recognize that we may waver in response to the fear of change.

## Unknown Outcomes

Sarah chose to stick with her earlier decision the second time around, in spite of having fallen irrevocably in love. Appreciating that she'll never know whether her decision was right or wrong she says: 'I learned things that will stay with me for the rest of my life and I did things that shaped who I am today.' So when asking yourself, 'Was that the right choice?' the truth is, you cannot be sure because you can never know how it would have turned out had you made a different choice. It seems that a 'good' or 'bad' decision may have either a 'good' or a 'bad' outcome. We just can't know beforehand. If you allow yourself to see the negatives as well as the positives when making a choice, it just becomes what it is, a choice with the possibility of many different outcomes.

Both storytellers talk about discovering the creative pursuits that they felt passionate about and the feelings that these discoveries generated. We believe that it is vital that we capture and remember these feelings when they occur. Those people who live life in order to replicate this self-realization will often tell you that this awareness is the secret of their happiness. We felt too, that it was really important to remember these feelings, but not to focus too much upon the specific cause, as similar feelings may flow from other sources. These feelings point the way to our happiness and natural self-expression, which, in turn, helps us to find meaning in our lives.

Both of these stories tell us how difficult it is to make important decisions. Both women acknowledged the dilemma they faced in making their choices and drew from the practical and rational, as well as their values and heart-felt instincts. We are often told, 'follow your heart' or 'follow your head', but real life is not that simple. We can see that integrating the two serves to satisfy a retrospective justification for their choices. What we mean by this is that in looking back, both Georgina and Sarah, even in their doubt, stood by their decisions and said that this integration served them well. However, when we're pressurised by well-meaning others, it is quite hard to hear these voices when they use practical, pragmatic, no-brainer logic!

As Sarah says, every cloud has a silver lining. In Georgina's story she found work that enabled her to be true to herself, even though it wasn't as an artist. Whatever route you take, you can find a way to express yourself – which is perhaps, the point of these two stories. We concluded that if you accept your choice with a positive disposition and a light heart, you get much more than you expected. In addition, you succeed in expanding your horizons, which are bound to hold more exciting possibilities in the long term.

CHAPTER 8
# A Matter of Purpose

This chapter tackles the issue of obligatory work versus heartfelt work. Most people spend a lot of their life at work and therefore, don't we owe it to ourselves to be working at what we love?

We have found three fantastic examples of people who talk about this dichotomy in their stories and reinforce the importance of this sentiment. Interestingly, they have found different ways of working this out, one of which may resonate with you. Also, significantly, all three of them talk of the importance of courage and self-confidence and recognize that this is often a huge developmental undertaking.

## Mark's story

Mark runs his own software design and development consultancy. As a gifted jazz guitarist, he lives in central London, where he has access to the city's musical scene. He has two grown-up daughters who, when young, lived with their mother a short distance away. We asked him to recall the time he was made redundant and the feelings that this induced in him, along with making a major life decision not to become a professional musician.

I was working for a company as a software development consultant. I worked from home mainly, but drove the four-hour journey to the office about once a fortnight. It was a great company to work for, it was doing really well and everything was going fine. Then, financial problems emerged and a new chief executive came in and set about the company with a sharp knife. He got rid of a lot of people. I survived this first round of redundancies and thought I'd probably be OK; but later that year, just after I had returned from a successful conference in San Francisco, the axe fell and the whole of my department was made redundant.

I was completely devastated! At that time I was 45 years old, and I was convinced I'd never get another job because I was too old. I had also been doing very specific work that I felt would reduce my employability, so I couldn't see a way out. Immediately, I cancelled the holiday I'd booked to Ireland with the girls, just out of sheer panic. I felt absolutely and completely dreadful!

After that, I spent all my energies trying to find another job. I applied for anything remotely suitable, drove all over the place and had a few interviews, but nothing particularly brilliant turned up. This confirmed my suspicions that I was too old, I was too specialized and the future really was incredibly bleak! Yet, even though I didn't feel very hopeful, I continued to do everything I could, 24 hours a day.

I went for jobs that were nothing like as good, or as interesting, or as well paid as the one I had lost, but I was just applying for anything at all. I was quite distraught about the situation and firing off applications in all directions. I do remember going to the job centre to sign on. When they asked what sort of job I wanted, I said I wanted a job like the one I'd lost and that I was going to find it without a problem. So outwardly, I was reasonably confident but of course, inside, I was feeling abject panic! I was thinking that I would never, ever work again! I realize this was a very extreme reaction. I was also supporting the girls, and there was the mortgage to pay, so I couldn't afford to wait. I had to get something soon, one way or another. So I worked up my CV and drove to all sorts of places.

At the same time, I was conscious that it wasn't a personal thing; it wasn't just me that had been made redundant, it was the whole department. This was very reassuring. Also, I had a colleague, locally, who was going through the same experience, so we were able to commiserate, compare notes, attend job fairs together and so on. It was really good to share this with somebody else and not feel completely isolated.

I've never really thought about what drove my need to work at that time, besides meeting my financial responsibilities. But thinking back, I really enjoyed working life. It was a good company to work for and I was able to work from home. They also gave me a great car and I travelled to the United States frequently. I felt confident. I felt connected to the outside world. I felt that I was doing something useful. I felt that I was somebody! When I was made redundant, these feelings disappeared altogether! I felt useless. I felt old. I felt as if I had lost all credibility as somebody who was not employed by the 'real world'!

Although I was looking for a full-time position, eventually, I discovered the world of contracting. How I never knew about this as an employment option before is a mystery to me! However, I explored this route and was eventually awarded a contract. This became my most significant decision at that time.

As a relatively successful part-time musician, I also made the choice at this time not to go professional. You might think it was an obvious option but I feel much more connected to a real, live enterprise through software development than I do through playing music. Even though they're both 'work', only software satisfies the criteria of being 'real' and 'live' at the same time. I have written and recorded several albums, and the two latest ones have quite a lot of potential. However, as neither of them are actually doing that well yet, the professional balance weighs in favour of software development. If these albums suddenly started to take off, I'm sure I would change the way I viewed the software work. It's all to do with feeling connected to work that I value and making a significant contribution, something that nobody else could do.

Music has always been part of my life. I started playing the piano when I was five years old and then, at 13, picked up the guitar, which I became obsessed with! I went on to play in bands at school and university. There have been two occasions when I had the opportunity to give everything else up and focus on music. One was at university, when the guys in the band wanted to ditch everything and go professional, but I said no. The second was when I was one half of a jazz duo and we were doing really well. We were both working full-time but in between, were doing gigs, radio and some television. My musical partner was prepared to give up his job to become a full-time musician but again, I said no.

On the first occasion, I decided not to chuck in my university studies because I was in the middle of my degree and maybe, too, I was lacking the confidence that I could be incredibly successful. There were other really good bands around my university at the time. There was Robert Palmer and Mick Ronson, both of whom were blatantly stars; and we weren't 'stars'. We played fairly well, but we were nothing like in their league. Of course, Robert Palmer went on to be an international superstar and Mick Ronson played with David Bowie for years and years. So I think I didn't believe that we could achieve anywhere near the same level of success. And also, my family ethos was all about being 'as safe as possible'. Just don't do anything that's vaguely unsafe or risky! So the most important thing was to get a 'safe job' at all costs – and I was not encouraged to play the sort of music I wanted to!

On the second occasion, with the jazz duo, it was because my daughters were really young, four and seven. I just thought it was too big a risk, financially, to make this commitment, and I would have had to travel all the time. Added to which, I had also been offered a full-time job, which I felt very positive about.

If, at university, we'd been in a band and David Bowie had asked us to go on a world tour with him for the next 12 months, perhaps it would have been different; the choice would have been much more obvious. Compared to this amazingly exciting opportunity, carrying on with the degree would have seemed very boring. The same applied to the jazz duo. If we'd got a gig in Paris for a month or a European tour or something, and if we had been really successful and were selling loads of albums and people really wanted to hear us... if that had been the case... Well, I may have made a different choice.

Now, it's all come round again. If my two albums make money and people say 'please write more music', it would give me such confidence and the ability to make a different choice – music over software development. I think there are others who make choices to follow their creative passions, whatever else is going on at the time. This is the antithesis of what I've been describing and I can't really relate to it, but I think it's obviously a very much more 'honourable' way of living.

If I'd had self-belief, I would done whatever it takes to be successful. But I would have needed to be sure that I was going to be good enough. For me, not having this level of self-belief was continually self-defeating. As long as I didn't put myself out there and really go for it, I was perpetuating the feeling that I wasn't good enough and sabotaging the chance of ever being so! I wouldn't say that I have regrets, but I would be very interested to watch an alternative lifetime video of what would have happened had I gone pro on either of these earlier two occasions.

However, having achieved my aim of being able to earn a decent living (quite a lucrative one latterly), I've put a lot more effort into my music and I'd hope that will continue. I'm very happy with this outcome.

In Georgina's story (Chapter 7: *A Matter of Perspective*), anticipating not being 'first rate' deterred her from choosing to become an artist. Mark, too, used this measure to choose software development over music. Both were parents who sought sound income-generating work over more risky, creative work – work that was their real passion and to which they returned with much more conviction later in life.

Georgina also said: 'Even though I was living my acquired values at that time, I'm glad [I made the choices I did] because I felt better about myself, although I sort of betrayed my true nature... I think now, I wish I had made more honest choices, but in fact it turned out to be a really good life to have and stood me in good stead.' Piecing together some of Mark's statements, the sentiment has a similar ring to it. 'The most important thing was to get a safe job at all costs... others who have creative passions make choices to follow them whatever is going on at the time... I wouldn't say that I had regrets, but I would be very interested to see an alternative lifetime video...'

Both acknowledged that they had put their passions in a second place to their 'acquired' values. Both felt it would be more 'honest' or 'honourable' to have followed their passions. But both saw the value in what they'd done and didn't really have serious regrets.

These stories demonstrate that you never lose a real passion that is part of you. The chances are that you will find an opportunity to express it at some time in your life. Georgina and Mark saw the value in courses they had chosen and didn't have serious regrets.

We're now going to introduce Emma and Jessica, who tell very different stories that nevertheless shed light on the issue getting in touch with what they really want to do. As we read these stories, we wondered how many other people in the world get caught up in what they perceive to be their obligations and end up compromising their dreams. We also identified very strongly with all of these storytellers, as we have both chosen to make major career changes in our professional lives, culminating in our choice to write this book.

In contrast with Mark and Georgina's cases, both Emma and Jessica had very high mountains to climb. Jessica fought a large corporation, very much on her own. Emma was isolated, holding on to a guilty secret for over four years. Yet both of these women followed their hearts and found real joy and satisfaction.

## Emma's story

Emma runs her own mental health business. It is growing rapidly and she feels that she is achieving her strategic and social aims. She juggles being a mother of three children with being a full-time chief executive, which requires her to work long hours and travel extensively. This is her story.

At the age of 37, I decided I wanted a family. I was away at a conference and it came to me when I was wallowing in the bath. I sent my husband a text just saying, 'I really want a baby', and he agreed it was time to start a family. I was the vice principle of a mental health authority at the time.

My first son was a real pleasure to me, so much so that I found myself wanting another child. Not only that but also, loving my sister as I did, I thought it would be a shame for him not to have a sibling.

The next few years were very traumatic as I suffered four miscarriages. Eventually I became pregnant with my second child and everything was fine and dandy until I went for a 28 week scan. Totally unexpectedly, they gave me the awful news that my baby son had died. And, in spite of this, I still had to give birth to my lovely boy.

I then fell into the deepest depression I could ever have imagined. I despaired that I would ever recover from the loss and go on to have another child. After a long, long time, when I began to feel a little brighter, we went away on holiday. When we returned I discovered I was pregnant. My son was two years old at this stage, and it came as a huge delight to me. I was ready again.

Because of my problematic medical history and because I was now 41, I was assigned to a renowned professor at the hospital. The first scan was fine. Then I went for the second scan, only to be told that I was carrying twins! The problem was that I was then in a constant state of trauma as I kept imagining that the babies' hearts had stopped beating. It was not an easy time. But the girls were born and I was very happy, grateful and fulfilled. There was my husband, my three wonderful children and me – a larger family than I had ever imagined.

Then I remember so clearly the day I was sitting on the sofa feeding my children; the sun was streaming through the window. I picked up a book someone had given me about women's spirituality and began to read it. Before I knew it, I found myself in floods of tears. I looked down at the children, my three wonderful gifts, and thought: 'I wonder if this is going to be enough for my mind and soul?' How could I even think such a thing!

To be honest, I truly adored and loved my children. They were everything, and more, than I had ever wanted. But deep down, I felt bored. My days and nights consisted of changing nappies, washing, breast feeding, getting the children to bed and then waking them up to feed them again. I was short on sleep and it was not very stimulating – I missed the challenge of work.

Most of my mum friends had not worked before having had their children, and they were not intending to go to work afterwards. So I pushed my thoughts of wanting to work away. I felt a real need to be grateful for my family and I tried to stop thinking about myself. This was reinforced every time I observed my friends, whose worlds were completely taken up with being a mum. I even began to believe that if I dared speak of my desires with anyone, my children would be taken away from me by some unforeseeable disaster. For these reasons, it became my own private secret. I lived with it for another two years.

During this time my choice became complicated and confused in my mind. Thinking about it by myself, I became afraid that my decision to have children meant that I had no further choices! I had three children and that was it! It was an 'all or nothing' choice!

I was really frightened about what others would say, because of the losses I had experienced. I could just hear them remarking: 'You would have thought that after all that she's been through, she'd want to spend time with her children!' I DID! But it was just not enough!

With my husband away quite often, I began to yearn for discussions on topics other than that of 'being a mum'. Then, one day, I found myself having a sort of 'different' conversation with another mother. As a result of this talk, we started up a small business. I stuck with it for some time but, if truth be told, it still did not provide me with the mental stimulation I craved.

Mums were – and still are – not comfortable with such feelings. I honestly felt that any mother who went back to work was judged to be a 'lesser' mother, certainly by the people with whom I mixed. I remember there was a period where I really tried to enjoy things that a 'good mother' should. I threw myself into playing Lego and reading children's books in an attempt to silence my doubts and deny my feelings, suppressing what I really thought.

In total, this went on for four years. Even now as I hear myself speak, I feel really guilty about it! The biggest pressure was being surrounded by people who seemed so fulfilled in their mothering, although I'll never *really* know if they were!

So in the end, I withdrew gradually from those people who had originally been such a great support to me. I could not identify so much with them anymore. Eventually, the choice that had been brewing for so long was forced from me because I had to go back to work for financial reasons. And, now that it was no longer a dream, I had to think really carefully about the consequences.

At first, I tried to focus on businesses that would exercise my intellect and could be run from home. Then I played with the idea of drawing from my experience and becoming a reader of legislation and policy for people in the NHS. I thought that was a great idea, because I knew they did not have the time to plough through all the documentation and I could prepare summaries for them. I had no end of ideas, but truthfully none of them excited me as I really wanted to be back in the classroom, training, and using my talents and skills again.

As life sometimes has it, one day when I was sitting on my sofa, my old boss knocked at the door. He was passing by and wondered if I wanted to consider doing some freelance consultancy. This was the most exciting thing anyone had said to me for four years!

So that's what I did! Gradually – and gratefully – I eased my way back into the world of work. At last I was able to be ME again, as well as being Mum. Even though my children are now 15 and 19, I can still feel guilty about making that choice, but I clearly needed to make it.

Only last week, when I was socialising with some old friends, they were talking about all the research they were doing on the best universities for their children. I have to say, I do not have the time to plough through so many details! However, when I hear about it from them, I begin to worry that I have not done the best for my children. I have had, and still have, my eye on another ball – namely work! You see? I'm compiling evidence against myself all the time!

Also, if either of my twins struggle at school or have difficulties with friends, it is easy for me to blame myself for this. This happens on a bad day. But on a good day, I see my children as being healthy, happy and fulfilled. I love them and I care for them. And I see us as a very balanced family. Because the girls and my son see me working really hard, and because they see the financial benefit of doing so, they are really passionate about finding jobs and earning money and being independent. I talk to them about balancing life, prioritizing their activities and attending to the important things. I try to be the best role model I can, knowing that 'just being a mum' would not have been enough for me. AND I think that my guilt in making my choice will probably never go away.

What making this choice did for me was to satisfy my yearning, which was not really shared by the mothers I was mixing with. Although it was hard for me to go against tradition and resist the pressure of what other people thought. When I had my first baby, I was catapulted into a world that I didn't know and I tended to measure myself by what others were doing. I suppose this is natural but it unnerved me. I know one woman who was a fantastic earth mother, was always there for her children; but now they are grown, she is really lonely. She spent 21 years away from the workplace and is really lost. So, what I'm saying is don't just be influenced by others' judgements. They may think they know what's right and wrong but I believe you never are THE ABSOLUTE RIGHT MUM, ever! In my view, there's no such thing as a good or bad way of being a mum; we simply do our best every step of the way.

In making my choice, I was able to hold on to a small part of me that is not called 'Mum'. I believe that

I'm fortunate because some mothers have not had the chance to find out who they are besides being a mum. In fact, I think those who don't work would probably find it difficult to understand the passion and rewards I get from working. For me, it's not about returning to work because I don't love my children, it's about what feels right for me; which in turn, gives all of us values and beliefs about work, family and individuality. The irony is that my choice may have developed some really special qualities in my children that otherwise would not have been possible. If that were the case, it would be a real gift coming from my decision. Perhaps it would even erase the guilt.... Hmmm, I doubt it!!

If I were advising someone in the same position, I'd say think very carefully about the logistics of work – time is at a premium and you have to be very organized. I'd also say get plenty of practical support so that you don't spend all your spare time cooking, cleaning and washing. Finally, I'd say don't be influenced by others' judgements. They are not yours.

Guilt is a very common emotion shared by many. As sensitive beings, guilt is an emotion we are good at wrapping around ourselves, yet we feel that it is an 'empty' emotion in that there is nothing positive to be gained from it and it saps our energy. We also remember from our youngsters' stories how we concluded that adults are good at making life over-complicated. As Emma has found, it is very easy to continually reinforce the evidence that underpins her guilt.

## Jessica's story

Jessica is a working mother who has a son at university. She works locally as the director of an arts charity, which teaches fine art print-making. In her story, she reflects on her experience of becoming disentangled from a large corporation, which had different career aspirations for her future to her own. She chose to fight her corner and, after considerable time and effort, she was able to create a new and fulfilling future for herself that maximized her talents.

I had been with a large corporate retail organization for over 20 years and it was an important part of my life, which I really enjoyed. I was the commercial head of the design studio for five years and had just finished implementing recommendations from a study that I had conducted when the announcement came that the department was to be split up. I loved my job and found it very difficult to accept the restructuring from a commercial standpoint, as well as a personal one. I was offered another position managing print procurement. It was a big job with a huge budget, but not in any way attractive to me or suited to my skills. I felt really disappointed and undervalued. I refused the position.

In an attempt to secure something more interesting and attractive, I set about trying to prove that the procurement job was 'smaller' than the one I had held previously. There followed quite a lot of tense meetings and negotiations but in the end, the point was ratified and it was agreed that I was not being offered like-for-like. However, I could see that even if

I stayed and did a different job, life would not be the same again. I had created a lot of ripples and many of my working relationships had suffered, so I concluded that perhaps it was time to leave.

Knowing the legalities of the situation, I asked the organization for a redundancy package. Unfortunately, they refused. This began a long fight, which lasted three months. I was standing up against a huge organization, and those I had considered my friends were loath to stand beside me for fear they would be drawn in. Apart from a very few loyal friends, I found it to be a very lonely place. For two months, I was obliged to go into the building, sit at my desk and turn on my computer. But I had no proper work to do because I didn't have a role! However, not only was I was convinced that I didn't want to take a backward step and do unfulfilling work, but also I was determined not to back down. So, I continued to be brave and I hung on until the end when eventually they gave me my redundancy. It was a fair sum of money and it would allow me to get organized and find something else that I wanted to do.

Leaving was a rational decision but my emotions were directed towards the people I would no longer see. I felt a huge sense of loss and injustice. The organization had changed a lot in the years I had been working there. It had been a company that treated its people very well and, in return, individuals gave real commitment. What's more, this consideration extended beyond the organization to each other. Now that it had all changed, I felt really sad.

I set about looking at the facts. I had been earning a very good salary but I had also spent a lot on travelling and employing a nanny for my son. I worked out that if I found a local job, I would still have a reasonable income and a better quality of life. This concerned my husband, who had seen my job as security for us – and especially for him – as he was not overly secure in his work. Also, he did not understand the emotional aspect of the decision at all. Also, my decision put him under more pressure to continue with his job. All this meant that I had to be really rational and calm when I presented him with the figures.

When the redundancy finally came through, I felt a huge sense of achievement – but then came the low! I was at home alone. My son was at school. My husband was at work. And I was under pressure to find a new job! I knew I had skills, but now that I had to use them to find another position, it was quite another matter. I decided that what I needed was structure, so I set about creating it.

As part of my leaving package I negotiated some outplacement support with a well-known company in London. So, I put on my suit and set off to attend workshops and meetings with my consultant, just as if I was going to work. I met other people in similar circumstances but to be honest, the workshop did not really teach me anything that I had not already learned during my career.

I decided to work the same hours that I was used

to working and I would focus on networking and job applications. I was determined to find something I really wanted to do that would allow me to use my commercial skills, but within a creative environment. One of the contacts I had was in the Royal Society of the Arts. I enjoyed talking to the creative people and joined a few other networks that were related to my area of interest.

I do remember feeling quite vulnerable at this time even though I knew I had something to offer. It was difficult finding the exact niche that I wanted to occupy. Also, having worked inside such a large organization for so long, I began to experience feelings of being less important. This really shook my confidence. But never for one moment did I think I had done the wrong thing! I mean, I could have stayed another eight to ten years and walked away with a good pension, but I couldn't see why I'd want to stay so long doing a job I didn't like just for that! It would feel like throwing my life away!

After a while, several artists asked me to become an agent for them. This was a turning point as I realized there were other ways of earning a living and other sorts of people out there. Building on this observation, I also gained confidence by going through a bespoke program with another person who was in the same situation as me. It was so good to meet someone who was going through similar emotions, someone with whom I could laugh with and share experiences. This was such a release, a great tonic and a big bonus.

We had to do a number of exercises, but the one I remember particularly well was writing life stories. I was very skeptical at first, but the stories soon began to flow and I found the process really cleansing. I began by writing about the major events in my life and then progressed to work. They covered things that I had enjoyed, things I felt I had failed at and things I felt I had achieved. Having been through such an emotionally charged period, I found it cathartic and helpful to empty out all the clutter. Then we shared our stories and picked out particular qualities that we noticed in each other's story. Some were professional attributes, but we also focused on personal traits, such as empathy or 'not suffering fools gladly'. We transferred these onto cards and gradually, as the exercise continued, we found we had gathered little mountains of qualities! It was great because when I looked at my little stack of cards, it gave me a real sense of 'who I am' and what I may be suited to.

To get the best out of the process, it was really important to feel relaxed and open. After all, if I had tried to hide, I wouldn't have reaped the benefit of the exercise. It was a fantastic experience. Through this, I confirmed that I like to work with creative people, support them commercially and undertake inventive projects. So, I focused my networking and job search in the arts. Shortly afterwards, when visiting with a local artist, I found myself being interviewed for a part-time position as the director of a newly formed arts charity aimed at teaching and promoting fine art print-making. I have now been there for 10 years and have built up the charity to the point where we're teaching students from five counties and have a huge adult education program. It is very rewarding working with people of all ages and experiences – and I love it!

This whole episode has made me realize that when working for the large organization that was my previous employer I wasn't recognized or appreciated properly. Looking back, I feel that I was being pushed down a path that did not match my skills or personal preferences. It is said that people perform best when they are happy and doing what they love to do, but more than this, it seems important for everyone's welfare.

The one thing I've learned from facing this difficult situation is how vital it is to be true to yourself. I believe you have to keep asking yourself, 'Do I believe in this?' and be resolute in your response. I think the stories were helpful in identifying my achievements and positive experiences. Through them, I was able to find confidence, especially when I shared them with others who were prepared to be supportive. But at the end of the day, you really are on your own. You have to make your own decisions, even though there will be times when they are not right. However, by being strong enough to admit mistakes, it is possible to rectify many choices; if you're open and receptive to change, you can get back on track and get on with life.

Mark and Jessica were reinforced in their feelings of confidence by their employers and, not surprisingly, they found their sense of identity through this. Their departure from these environments triggered a need to take responsibility for building their own confidence and find a self-sufficiency that they had previously not enjoyed.

## Standing Alone

The self-awareness and understanding of 'who you are', without any attachment to a professional establishment, is where Emma's story links with Mark and Jessica. She found that her identity as a mother was not sufficient to satisfy her calling or nourish her self-esteem. This resulted in the choices she discussed above.

We can see that when you know yourself well, and when you hold dreams that are aligned to your true nature, the perfect opportunities come knocking on your door. Perhaps those opportunities are always there. Whatever the case, when we tap into the potential that they offer with confidence, they enable us to find new ways to succeed and be happy.

In ending this chapter, we thought it might be helpful to ask whether you have ever dared to dream? And, if not, how about using the technique that Jessica describes and discover the 'little mountains' that catalogue your talents and ambitions?

In the words of one of Dena's favourite singers:

'You're never more than a step away from having everything you've wanted.' (Glen Hansard, 'The Swell Season')

# CHAPTER 9

# A Matter of Simplicity

This chapter is one of our favourites because it includes stories by children and young adults. We had not expected some of their statements to be quite so provocative and wise, which as with all the stories, have been preserved in their original form. When we approached these youngsters, we were curious to see if choices felt simpler to them. However, as a result of our discussions, this has not necessarily turned out to be the case.

## Lily's story
Lily, aged 15, related our first story. She lives with her

parents, older sister and younger brother in a town on the periphery of London. As a middle child, she has found distinction through a passion for outdoor sports, especially (and perhaps unusually for a girl) playing rugby, a game she plays to county level.

Okay, when you first told me about this, I was stumped. I thought, 'I'm 15, what big choices have I ever had to make?' But after thinking about it, I realised that all the little choices I've had to make have made all the difference, whether to me personally, or to things around me.

The first important choice I remember having to make was whether to go to the rugby training I had been invited to earlier in the week. I had played for the school team, and loved it, but being in Year 7, I was still a bit shy of meeting new people. I remember staying in my bedroom quietly till 7.30, when the training started at 7.00; so I could just 'accidently' have missed it. My dad soon found me, and said, 'Come on then, are we going to rugby?' And I made the excuse that we would be too late. He didn't push me, but he could see that I was undecided as to whether I wanted to go or not. I knew right inside I wanted to go, so I timidly said, 'Okay then'. Then my dad got straight up, not letting me change my mind. That 'Okay then' was the best decision I have ever made. Three years on, I have found what I want to do for the rest of my life. I have changed as a person, and the friends I have made are friends I could never imagine I would have had.

This experience made me understand that the best way to go was to 'Just do it!' My confidence has grown all round. I can speak in public to large groups and I got an 'A' grade in my oral speech in GCSE English. This is something I never thought I would be able to achieve. Rugby has provided a place where I could choose to try different things and test my strengths and weaknesses. Now I have been able to bring that confidence from the rugby pitch and into school and my social life.

When I started playing matches, my original game was to get the ball, and run straight down the line. Don't get me wrong, it worked, but now I have developed my game into so much more. I didn't have the confidence at first, but when I chose to put my 'Go for it!' attitude into play, I decided to kick, decided to cut in lines, decided to just floor the girl running towards me with no second thoughts. Well, I'm now playing above regional levels! This has also shown through in my schoolwork, but I didn't realise until recently. My grades have been so much stronger, because I have had the confidence to say to myself, 'You can do this!'

Another decision I remember having to make was when the PGL (Parents Get Lost!) letters were sent out. (These are letters that invite pupils on school trips.) I was sitting in class with one of my best friends and we decided we wanted to go on the trip. It was a lot of money, but looked really fun. No one else we knew terribly well was going, but we decided that we didn't want to be sheep and not go, just because others were not. We talked about it and then the next week we handed our money in. I was really glad we did this, as it was something different we could do together; a lot of the time we were doing the same old stuff with the same group of people.

The trip was planned about half a year ahead, so when I agreed to go, I didn't have anything else in the diary. However, later on I found out that on the Saturday of the long PGL weekend I was due to play my last rugby tournament of the season. I wouldn't be playing with the girls in the team for another year, and it was a 'Sevens' tournament, the one that I enjoy the most. I was gutted! I didn't have a clue what to do. The trip was all paid for and non-refundable and I really didn't want to let my friend down, as it would be like leaving her on her own if I didn't go. I didn't even want to talk to her about it, as I thought she might feel like I was on the verge of choosing rugby over her. I talked to the girls at rugby and they told me to go on the PGL trip – they said that I would have so much fun, and that I would definitely have the chance to play rugby with them again. I still couldn't make up my mind, and I even tried writing down 'reasons to go' and 'reasons not to go' on my whiteboard with my mum.

The advice my rugby friends gave me soon got to me and I understood that if I had made a decision, I shouldn't back out of it. If I chose to go a couple of months ago, I knew that at some point it was exactly what I wanted, so I should be glad I had the chance to go on a weekend full of high ropes, canoeing, zip wiring and so much more. I knew I would have many more chances to play in a rugby match with my team mates. I was just being self-centred and didn't want to miss out on anything.

I went on the trip, and had such a good time, doing things that I can't imagine having the chance to do again. I was so glad I went instead of going to the rugby tournament, as the year has already sped by, and I will be playing with my old team again. I did mention it to my friend though, and told her everything that had happened. She said that she wouldn't have minded that much, but she was really glad I came. It showed me that if I were to do it again, I should speak to her and get her opinion. Not asking her just showed me that that I didn't really want to know what she'd say because I knew that I should go on the trip. I know I made the right decision, since even though I feel I may have missed a few things, those opportunities will come round again.

## Push and Pull Factors

We're going to break Lily's story here to return to the important concept of the 'push' and 'pull' dynamic in choice-making. Lily comments that her Dad 'didn't push' her to go to rugby training, but it appears that he gave her the courage to say 'yes' by giving her the time and space to make the choice for herself. Then he 'got straight up', making it possible for her to act on her decision before she could change her mind. In what seemed to us a brilliant stroke of parenting he compelled her to take responsibility for what she wanted and then supported her in the decision she made.

We talked about the difference between choices that are made as a result of 'push' and 'pull' influences in Georgina's story. This passage, we felt, was another illustration of the 'pull' influence and the way it can affect choice. Lily was 'pulled' in the direction of her desire through her father asking a pointed question and then allowing her to come up with her own answer. She was not forced into doing something that she may have felt angry about or resented later. Nor did he try to persuade or influence her. He enabled her to get to the place of choice for herself and she made her own decision as a result of this, one that felt entirely right for her.

At this point, we also want to introduce a new concept, the *turnkey* phrase. Lily's simple and straightforward 'Just go for it!' formula enabled her to develop into 'so much more'. In Mary's story (page 64), Emily's response to the situation was similar. She said, 'Live with it Aunty Mary!' These are good examples of turnkey phrases: short, effective expressions that encapsulate simple ways of approaching next steps. These ideas represent uncomplicated actions that unlock and open a door to new skills, capabilities and attitudes. In Lily's case, the valuable spin-off from acting on this turnkey phrase was an increase in self-confidence, which not only translated into great grades in her schoolwork, but also enabled her to find something that she may be passionate about for a long time to come.

We were interested in Lily's comment about not talking to her best friend about her dilemma. She noted that if this type of situation arose again, she would ask for her friend's opinion. How often do we make things difficult for ourselves by thinking we know what someone else's reaction will be? These judgements, made without real knowledge of the facts, can inhibit or sabotage us, and could even prevent us from making life-changing decisions.

Going back to Lily:

I think that the choice I am currently making is lot different to the ones I have made in the past. I've just had a music audition; it was to move up to the concert band, which is the top of the music school. I wasn't given the choice to make the move. During one lesson, my music teacher said: 'This is the piece I think you should do for the audition.' I was stumped! I only had a week to prepare and I wasn't keen on going. My friend definitely decided she didn't want to do it, so I thought I'd do the same as her. But suddenly I was attending the audition! I didn't have much confidence and the only reason I eventually agreed to do it was because I didn't want to let my teacher down, even though she was leaving the week before and wouldn't know whether I had completed it or not.

I was put into a room to warm up, and the only thoughts that were going through my head were: 'That window is definitely big enough to jump out of!' It was the ground floor, don't worry – I wasn't considering suicide... just escaping! I kept telling myself that it would be over in 20 minutes and I had nothing to worry about, but that didn't help. I was called into the exam room and was asked to play my piece. I didn't make any mistakes and got through it fine. I was then asked to do sight reading and this was my downfall. I just panicked because they gave the music to me on white paper. I have mild dyslexia – when reading music on white paper the notes just glare at me and move around on the page. However, using green paper allows me to read the music with less trouble.

I played through it though, and gave my best. I did read it incorrectly in places, but the examiners told me where I went wrong. The second time I managed to do a bit better. I was unbelievably nervous all through the audition. I hated every second of it. However, I was successful. The examiners told me that they loved my playing and said that I would fit in fine with the upper band. I was so happy. I had done it and battled through the nerves. However, they did tell me I should see an optician about my dyslexia and get coloured glasses so I could read more easily. I don't like telling people about it. I feel that people might think I'm acting dyslexic or that I'm stupid. I don't want to make a big deal and let people know about my condition, so I think I'll talk to my optician and see whether she can make glasses where you can barely see the green tint. Or maybe I'll get contact lenses. If they can't though, I'm sure that in time I will realize that it shouldn't matter what people think, and that if it helps me, I should 'Just do it!'

Now, I try to look at everything with the attitude that, 'If it doesn't kill you it makes you stronger' – and I love it! My choices are made so much easier because if I want to do something, or feel I should do something, I do it. I think that to regret something is the worst feeling ever. Thinking that, 'I could have done that', is the worst kind of feeling. I do everything I can to avoid regrets. If the choice you make doesn't turn out how you'd like, you always know that you've tried.

We both remember feeling pressurised into doing something because not doing it would have felt like letting down someone who was important to us. Lily shows great awareness of her own feelings and the feelings of those close to her. We see this 'other awareness' again later in this chapter and its importance in shaping a choice.

### Ruby's story

Our next story comes from Ruby, who is not quite 12 – although her tender age does not stop her having strong opinions, as you will see! She lives at home with her mother and younger brother and shows signs of being an assertive teenager with all the usual distractions and desires. Here are her thoughts about choices she has made in the school environment.

A big decision for me was choosing how to participate in lessons when I first went to high school. It felt like a huge step because I wasn't used to being in such a big school. I worried about what the teachers would be like and whether I would cope with the work.

My first choice was whether to put my hand up in class on the first day. It was very scary because I didn't know anybody, and I thought if I got something wrong, the teacher would tell me off and I'd feel embarrassed. Also, I was worried that my classmates would tease me. But, because the person sitting next to me (Karen) looked confused, I made a choice and I put my hand up. When I did, she said, 'I didn't understand that either!' So I thought it's not really so bad to put your hand up, because others are probably thinking the same as you. And anyway, the teacher would probably ask people at random and if I didn't speak up, she'd probably choose me! So I thought I might just as well put my hand up. At the end, when we were walking out, Karen said, 'Thanks for asking that question. I didn't want to put my hand up in case people teased me!' And I said, 'You should always put your hand up if you don't understand something.' I'm glad I did put my hand up, because if I hadn't, I'd have probably sat at the back and not got involved as much.

We've just had sports day at my high school and we were allowed to choose whether to participate in the events or not. If you chose not to participate, you could take a walk. If you did participate, you could run in the relay race and do some of the other activities. I thought that if I didn't take part at all, our house wouldn't be able to win the sports day, so it turned out to be quite an important choice. I ended up doing the tug-of-war and some of the other activities, and I did run in the relay. I decided to participate because I thought it didn't really matter if I did badly – at least we'd get some points!

In the morning activities I contributed some ideas to the exercises, which meant that we had a better chance of winning. I thought we might win if I spoke up and if I didn't, we'd probably lose. Even though I had done one of the exercises before, I was worried that people would laugh at me if they didn't like my idea – but the thought of winning made me brave. We won both activities.

Earlier, Lily gave a commentary on her feelings about her dyslexia. Her sensitivity and awareness of the pros and cons of her condition and the courage with which she approached it was admirable. Ruby talks about raising her hand in class as being '...very scary because I didn't know anybody, and I thought if I got something wrong, the teacher would tell me off and I'd feel embarrassed.' She also went on to say: 'I was worried that my classmates would tease me.' Both these anecdotes demonstrate self-awareness. It struck us how significant it was to both Lily and Ruby that in making their choices they would be seen and judged by those in positions of authority and importance. At a young age, both girls are acutely aware of how others might perceive them. Self-awareness and openness to input from others forms a really big part in helping youngsters develop their confidence and form their personalities, deciding how they want to be in the world. It was a real reminder to us to be mindful about how we choose to respond to them.

Also, Ruby deduced that 'It's really not so bad to put your hand up, because others are probably thinking the same as you.' How astute is that?! And also, what a great way of building up courage. Her friend Karen said: 'Thanks for asking that question', which affirmed Ruby's actions and gave her the confidence to keep on doing what she had chosen to do in that moment. Isn't affirmation an important element in all our lives?

We asked Ruby to think about some hard choices and how she'd approach these. This is how she responded:

A hard choice would be what to do if I was being bullied at school. I'd probably not know what to do because if I go and tell the teacher, it'd probably get worse. So, I'd tell a friend instead and see what she says. But she'd probably say, 'Oh you must go and tell your tutor or your head of year.' And I'd say, 'No, because I'm scared the bullies could do something else to me!' But my friend would probably go with me and it would get sorted out. I think choices are much easier if there's somebody else involved and you get some support. Like if I was making a choice about which exams to sit, I'd talk to my teacher and say I'm thinking of doing the exam and ask if they think I should do it. If they reply, 'You should give it a go', then I'd probably say, 'Alright!' And if my other friends were doing it, I'd probably do it, too.

This is another example of how important encouragement is in assisting choice-making, especially for the young. In Lily's story, her father played this part, and Ruby speculated that this would be important. Moving on:

If somebody was encouraging me to do something I didn't want to do, like smoking, I'd probably tell my head of year, because I know it's not good for you. Wherever you go, you see loads of adverts saying you should stop smoking because it might affect your heart and lungs and you might die from it. So, because of all this information, it would probably be the right decision to go and tell. If I didn't have this information, I'd probably go and ask somebody who knew anyway.

So, as we can see, when in doubt, research helps you work it out!

The sorts of decisions I make by myself are things such as deciding what to have for lunch. I can either choose something that's fatty and unhealthy or something that's healthy. Most of the time, I go for something healthy and then, when I get home, I might have a little chocolate bar or something as a reward! But mainly I eat something that's healthy. The other day at school I had fish and chips with no salt or vinegar. Instead, I had lemon on top. So it was sort of healthy, because fish is a healthy food for your brain, and then it had lemon on top of it, and the chips were flavourless, so they were probably healthy too. And without salt or vinegar – or cheese!

Some choices have really long-lasting consequences, such as eating junk food. If you eat junk food you'll be really unhealthy – and it's important to be healthy because it's easier to be cured from diseases. If you're really unhealthy it's harder to be cured and you may die!

Thinking about how she influenced others' choices, Ruby had this to say:

If Jake (my brother) had a choice of eating a peach or a packet of crisps, I'd say, 'Jake, go for the peach because it's healthy; if you have a packet of crisps, you'll probably get really addicted to them.' Because, with some crisps, you have one and then you want another and then you want another and then you want another! So I'd probably say to Jake, 'Just have the peach because it's healthy, and if you have too many crisps, you'll get really horrible and fat!' I don't know why you want more and more crisps. It's probably because of the nice flavour. I liked the caramelised onion flavoured ones, but when I have one, I just want another and another! I think the makers do that to sell more.

Reflecting on the general subject of choice, Ruby has this to say:

I think choices are important because they can change your life. If you don't ask that important question in class and it comes up in an exam, you might miss a really important mark that will stop you from going to college. I think all choices matter, whether they are big or small. Even choosing a peach instead of a packet of crisps can affect your whole life in the long term.

When I make my choices I think about being healthy and being kind – because people will probably be kind back to you! And I think it's important to be honest – because if you lie you'll get found out and get into trouble. You can't get away with doing something without anybody seeing, especially in school, because there are CCTV cameras around.

I don't think it matters what other people think: but then again, I think it does. Like, for example, if people believe in God and I don't. Then I'd think they've got their own point of view and I've got my own point of view. I do respect people's point of view and then again, I value my own. The only time I'd really care what other people think is if I was putting my life at risk.

I also try to think positively. I tell myself that nothing really bad can happen. In fact, the worst thing that's going to happen is that I will be teased, and I can always tell the teacher if this happens! So, if I was advising somebody who was having difficulty making a choice, I'd say to them, just be brave and do what you need to do – and find support.

At the tender age of 11, Ruby is already able to be very balanced in the way she views others' choices. She says: 'I think they've got their point of view AND I've got my own point of view!' Acknowledging that others may see things differently to us, yet still being able to hold our own counsel, requires confidence and shows a sophisticated outlook. The strategy that Ruby adopts of thinking positively and looking at the broad picture, where she talks about 'the worst thing that's going to happen', is also great preparation for some of the major decisions she's going to have to make in her life.

We're now going to turn to a light-hearted anecdote from a 13-year-old girl, Lizzie, who also considers the worst case scenario when finding courage to make a decision.

When I was seven, I went to Australia to visit family and to do all sorts of cultural things. We were in the Daintree Rainforest and the guide, who was showing my family around, was talking about a type of ant that had a yellow-coloured bottom. He said that Captain Cook, or whoever, had licked the ant's bottom to get vitamin C to stop scurvy, and that it tasted like lemon. Then he offered a sweet to whoever licked the ant's bottom, and I wanted a sweet so I looked at the ant and its yellow bottom and thought: if somebody else has done it, why shouldn't I? And the worst that can happen is that it will taste disgusting! So I licked the ant's bottom and it did taste like lemon. My brother went 'Urrggghhh!' Then he thought that if he licked the ant's bottom, he would get a sweet too, so he did; but he didn't get a sweet, because he hadn't gone first!

So, in conclusion, we found that the youngsters we interviewed did not find making choices an easy or simple process. Often the choice felt difficult, with them feeling the weight of others' opinions pressuring them to do the right thing. Yet they found straightforward, smart strategies to enable them to take the plunge and just get on with life, and they were able to be detached about the outcomes and learn from their experiences.

These turnkey phrases helped them make courageous decisions and experience themselves growing stronger:

'Just be brave and do what you have to do!'

'If it doesn't kill you, it makes you stronger!'

'If I want to do something… I do it!'

'If somebody else has done it, why shouldn't I?'

'The worst that can happen is….'

Amazingly, they were even able to go beyond that. Lily

goes on to say that her choices are made so much easier now, because if she wants to do something, she does it, citing regret as the 'worst possible feeling ever!'

We reflected that as adults how easily we can make things unnecessarily complicated. A profound thought! And this is why this is one of our favourite chapters.

# CHAPTER 10

# A Matter of Recovery

Jane has been on a long journey and has written this inspiring story about recovering from alcoholism. As a result of a chronic physical illness, which took her out of the workplace in February 2008, she is now working on a pain management programme – a programme she feels could not have been successful without the tools she acquired in recovery.

## Jane's story

Jane is the mother of accomplished twin girls and a son who works as a successful chef. Her marriage, sadly, ended in divorce. She aspires to set up as a freelance administrator in the rural business sector, running her own business in order to accommodate the limitations of her illness, which sometimes reaches debilitating levels.

My ego, the source of my personal desires and insecurities, was what caused me to seek solace in alcohol. My greatest difficulty has always stemmed from my emotional over-sensitivity and my skewed perceptions of my self-importance.

Initially, drinking alcohol seemed to give me confidence, raising self-esteem and creating feelings of being 'normal' that I had never previously experienced. Unlike non-alcoholic drinkers, who recognize when to stop drinking because they don't enjoy the feeling of being out of control, I felt the opposite. Instead of saying, 'I've had enough', as most people do when they start to get a bit tiddly, I kept on drinking. I did so because I already felt that my life was out of control and I felt that alcohol actually *gave* me a degree of control because, after all, I was choosing it. And it meant that I felt able to function without the seemingly inherent feelings of inadequacy and the inability to 'fit in' that dogged my life.

I say 'seemingly' because it was a fantasy. It was not really true. It was a belief I allowed to creep in because of the judgement of others. The messages came from people who I saw as being in authority: my mother, for instance, and teachers; also my ex-husband. The messages tended to suggest that I was unable to cope, that 'she couldn't do this and she couldn't do that!'

Making sense of it from where I am now, I guess they did this because they were projecting their own insecurities upon me. And I co-operated with them inasmuch as I accepted the 'victim' role. I really did believe that my mother was right about what she saw as my shortcomings and I felt especially lacking when she said, with a long suffering tone, 'Why can't you be like your sisters?!'

So, while the rest of my family (and my friends) seemed to have a natural defence against 'destructive messages' from people in authority, I took all of these on board and accepted them as the truth. At the same time, I never seemed to hear any messages of affirmation nor positive remarks about my personality, assets, competencies and skills, although I am aware, in hindsight, that these messages did in fact outnumber the negative ones. This meant that all my life, other people's negative opinions shaped my path – I was defined by what I believed other people thought of me. I was constantly trying to win their approval, affection and respect, not understanding that sometimes, it would have been better to dismiss their comments rather than taking them literally. I see now, that I didn't really understand that people have 'bad hair days' and that sometimes, their comments and opinions had nothing to do with me. I just believed it all!

Under the influence of alcohol I developed a false bravado. This helped me to sustain the fantasy that I was the person I thought I wanted to be. My imagination ran wild and I saw myself as a defender of the faith, a martyr for innumerable causes; infamous, a celebrity, a STAR! The problem was that I was incapable of achieving such dizzy and grandiose heights. I was never a grafter. I always expected that what was in my imagination would be automatically given to me without effort. I never considered that I needed to apply myself.

Stopping me from taking responsibility for my own life stood fear of failure, loneliness and a sense of personal inadequacy – all traits adopted by swallowing others' opinions whole. Nevertheless, I did not feel capable of looking after myself, getting a job and finding myself a place to live.

I married to escape. A consequence of my decision was that I needed to practice 'give and take'. I was more than happy to take the security as my due, without any thought of reasonable commitment on my part; and certainly no gratitude for the provision granted me by my husband.

I divorced to escape. I had adopted a victim role in order to survive what I believed were my husband's abusive, unreasonable and demanding ways. Despite my fixed ideas that the amount I drank was relative to the way I felt as a supposed 'used, abused and taken for granted' wife, my use of alcohol continued to escalate after the divorce.

Two years later, I repeated the pattern by rushing into a new relationship, selling my house and blowing the proceeds on compulsive shopping habits and a secret stash of alcohol. I hit an emotional, mental and physical rock bottom. My partner had the courage to evict me for my behaviour and my out-of-control drinking, which was, by this time, to counteract the emptiness and despair I felt.

So, aged 50, I found myself with my parents again, reliving what I believed to be a persecuted childhood with people who 'didn't understand'. I returned to the bottle and ended up suffering from all the accompanying phobias and panic attacks. My health was deteriorating and I didn't want to go on living – but I was terrified of dying.

I took an overdose. My parents were out at the time and came back to find me in a woozy state. However, I was alert enough to hear my mother say to my father: 'She's gone too far. I can't cope with this any longer. She can't stay here anymore.' It was then that I realized how selfish and ungrateful I had been. All the other losses – being homeless, unemployed and unemployable – anything material – didn't have the same significance as realizing that I'd sunk so low that I was abusing the people who were trying to help me.

The full extent of this truth finally hit me and I had deep feelings of remorse. My family had run out of patience. I was about to lose the only thing that I had left, my immediate family; the only people who had always been there for me despite my behaviour. I knew I had no alternative but to begin taking control – this time for real. At this point, I made the best and hardest choice I have ever made. I went to Alcoholics Anonymous (AA). That was more than six years ago. I have not drunk alcohol since then.

People think that alcoholics are incredibly weak. What I discovered, through AA, is that I'm incredibly strong. After all, I had the will to drive myself to the off-licence over and again, when I should have been in hospital! Before my recovery began, I used my strength destructively, not only against myself, but also against those I loved. Now I use my strength creatively.

My journey has not been an easy one. I have had to become completely honest about my feelings, my fears and my shortcomings. I have had to focus on my faults and learn humility as I took the first painful steps of letting go of the unhelpful ideas that I had allowed to rule my life and influence my choices. I had to draw upon a resource deep within myself; one that I hadn't tapped before.

I used to see 'God' as something awesome and frightening outside myself. It didn't occur to me that there was something divine within me. Once I understood this, I learned how to listen to it. Actually, I'd call it my conscience, and it is much more powerful than my ego. (It is also much more powerful than alcoholic drink!)

I accessed this part of myself through prayer and meditation, and I also employed the strategy of 'Fake it to make it'! In *The Big Book* of Alcoholics Anonymous, it says: 'It is easier to act yourself into a new way of thinking than to think yourself into a new way of acting.' I have yet to find a better or simpler description of 'Fake it to make it', or 'Acting as if.....'. It has certainly worked for me on many occasions. For example, with a family relationship, if I behaved as if everything was OK and didn't say what I thought (fake it!), I got a better response (make it!). I didn't realize that the negativity that I was receiving from others was a direct result of what I was giving out. When I changed this (falsely to begin with), the response I received also changed.

By doing this, I learned to become more responsive and less reactive. Not because I was in a responsive state of mind (in fact, my head may have been telling me to behave in a crazy way), but because I could see the value of it and it seemed like the 'right thing' to do; it satisfied my conscience. Then I felt comfortable with myself: no empty hole in the gut; no adrenalin rush due to feelings of guilt. So, the 'play acting' helped me learn how to achieve my ends. I must say, a lot of it was accidental, through trial and error.

Saying mantras to empty my head of unhelpful thoughts and become fully present was a tool I used successfully. This stopped the constant chatter in my head and helped me to live in the moment.

When I first went into recovery, I found I had become many people, each one trying to please all the different people in my life, all engaged in mental dialogue and vying for position. Because of the sheer number of demands, it was impossible to please everyone. It was very confusing! But I learned to sort out the noise and become one person. And I recognized the power within me, which gave me meaning and hope.

Now I feel that I have exchanged a malevolent power for a benevolent power. The very same feelings that were terrifying to me in the past now guide how I live my life. I used to be pretty poor at standing up for myself because I was too busy fighting imaginary demons to tackle issues directly. Today, although I know I can't control all the challenges that I encounter, I do feel able to change my attitude towards them and experience a different outcome. Driving in heavy traffic is a good example. In the past, if I were held up by traffic, I would probably end up driving dangerously by flooring the accelerator and weaving in and out of the cars in my way. Damn them! I'd think. Now, I'm learning to use my inner resources to keep calm. It works mostly, and if it doesn't, at least I understand what's going on inside me and can make choices about how to deal with it. All of these developments have enabled me to be more assertive and I've found a new respect for myself.

These are my choices – and they could become yours:

- I choose to attend AA meetings because I want to.
- I choose to remember that I am human being, who experiences disappointment; that I do get hurt; and that I am vulnerable and far from perfect.
- I choose to be as honest as I can be about myself.

- I choose my friends with care.
- I choose to continue to ask for help from those whom I trust, and sometimes I choose to take their advice.

The result of all these choices is a sense of emotional and spiritual balance, which affords me peace of mind. Today, I choose not to drink. I live for today. I am a good friend to myself.

## The Point of Choice

There is so much about choice in this extraordinary story. However, because we understand that alcoholism is such a complex condition, we have chosen to focus upon something we call the 'point of choice'. Not only does this mean the *purpose* of the choice being made, but also the point, or time, at which the choice becomes *unavoidable* and *has* to be made. We might also call it the 'point of realisation'.

In Jane's story, she finally 'knew' that she had to take control when she overheard her mother saying, 'She's gone too far. I can't cope with this any longer. She can't stay here any more.' At this point, she knew that she was being 'selfish and ungrateful' and undermining those who were trying to help her. These descriptions were everything she abhorred in herself and they triggered a response that led her into a journey of recovery. Those words were sufficiently charged to bring her to the point of no return.

All the strategies that she used to maintain her alcoholism – which she saw as enabling her survival – fell away, and she was compelled to take up the reigns and steer the course of her own life. Of course, others' stories have also pinpointed this place in the choice-making process. Remember Emma, who looked at her babies and suddenly realised that being a full time mum was not enough. Remember Barbara, who upon seeing the duck on the dinner table, thought: 'No. I just won't be a part of this!'

It is remarkable to note that all the stories pivoted on a point of convergence, when each person's history crystallised at a particular moment in time and presented them with the impetus to choose a new direction. This history, which included all those times when we have colluded with ourselves in 'choosing not to choose', builds a powerful momentum, which takes huge commitment to arrest. After this critical part of the process has been reached, the qualities of courage and stamina are crucial in moving forwards. In Jane's story, she talked of going to Alcoholics Anonymous – which is a smart way of helping her find the inner resources and support to enable her to maintain her new path.

This sense of resolve comes to us at different points in our lives; it is crucial to recognize and understand this feeling in order to apply our learning to help us navigate into the future and become the arbiter of our own destinies.

CHAPTER 11
# A Matter of New Beginnings

As this book has unfolded, we feel as if we've been walking alongside our storytellers, in the spirit of companionship. In doing this, we hope we have plotted a route that has encompassed many circumstances and many different types of choice; and we hope, through the voices of others, that we have managed to distil some ideas that will throw light on some of the choices you may be presented with in the future. Again, may we remind you to take inspiration from the stories rather than use them as a blueprint for decision making.

We felt, however, that we couldn't end this project without

acknowledging the different kinds of choices that people have to make when there is no choice. To achieve this, we'd like to introduce Margaret, who recounts a story of life-changing proportions. We think you'll agree that Margaret embodies great courage and pragmatism as she chooses to rebuild her life after losing her beloved husband to cancer.

## Margaret's story

Margaret has two grown-up daughters and six grandchildren. She lives in the countryside in a beautiful Tudor farmhouse (a family home that requires a lot of upkeep and attention).

This account tells of some of the trauma that my late husband and I went through during his long illness. He died of prostate cancer nearly two years ago, and I still find it painful to recall the events of the last few years of his life. Happily, however, these memories are gradually being replaced by happier ones of our life together before his illness was discovered, seven years before his eventual demise.

I had to make a conscious decision not to let myself fall into depression and lethargy following his death, so I took positive steps to join in with activities where I might meet others with similar interests and experiences. This has paid off and I am now in the lucky position of having found a special man-friend.

At the time of the diagnosis, I didn't really appreciate what was going on. It was all too overwhelming. But what I did know was that this disease would take David away from me and I was terrified of not being equal to the task of nursing him and being present at his death. However, with the help of the National Health Service and Macmillan Cancer Support, we were able to ease his path as the disease took hold, spreading eventually to his bone marrow and confining him to a wheelchair. And I did manage to keep him at home until the very last days, a fact of which I am immensely proud.

After his initial diagnosis, he responded well to the battery of treatments he received, and our hopes were high. But soon afterwards, one-by-one they failed, and dashed our hopes of total remission. The form of cancer he suffered from was very aggressive and it reappeared, initially, in the kidney. Because his life expectancy was so short, the oncologists were in two minds whether or not to remove it. David, however, was determined to live for as long as possible and insisted on the operation. The oncologist in charge of the treatment eventually agreed to the operation, saying that he expected David to live for at least another year as a result of it. And he joked that he had better not let him down by dying before then! David and he were always joking together – it seemed the only thing to do. After the kidney was removed, David lived another four years. Although he was fearful of dying, he never showed it and was always in good spirits.

David had a fantastic array of books in his library, which was situated on the ground floor of our house. When he could no longer climb the stairs, this became his bedroom. He was devoted to his books, collected at great expense over the course of his adult life. They gave him a sense of security and identity. How he loved them!

Then one day, as we were nearing the full crisis of his illness, I asked him if he would like to choose one of his many books to read – I said I would read aloud for him. 'What books?' he said! I waved my hand towards the bookshelves and replied: 'You know, all your lovely books over here in your library.' But he couldn't see them. He just said: 'But there's a lovely view down to the water, isn't there?' It was a real shock to me but I knew it meant that he must be nearing the end and that the hospice would not present such a nightmare to him as it previously had done. So he went in for the first time. He had several episodes of a week or 10 days in the hospice, and each time he seemed to get a little better and they sent him home again. He never complained.

The day he died, I received a phone call early in the morning – I had gone home late the previous night to snatch an hour or two of sleep, as David couldn't bear to be without me for long. I was asked to come in immediately, as he was sinking. My daughter joined me at his bedside later on. When I saw him, he was still just breathing, with short heavy breaths at regular intervals. They told me that although he could still probably hear my voice, he could not respond in any way, nor could he see me. I held his hand, which was warm and smooth, and we stayed like that for hours. I knew he needed to give in and let go, but he just didn't seem able to do it. I said, 'It is all right to go. I will see you again one day, I promise.' He still did not seem to want to go, and I suddenly realized he was worrying about what was going to happen to me when he had gone, so I said: 'You needn't worry, Lucy is here with me and will look after me. You can go now and rest.' And with that he took his last breath.

They laid him out in his best suit, and although he looked pale, he looked just as I remember my dear husband. I was fine at this stage and didn't shed a tear. As I drove home, I looked at the pale winter sky; as the sun set over the fields, I thanked God that it was all over. The relief was overwhelming.

My friends helped me organize the funeral and his children from his former marriage arrived from overseas. It was a very busy time but the funeral went off well. I was beautifully supported and I was coping well. I resorted to reading books – all my old favourites – and lost myself in the stories they told. Sometimes, I'd watch a gentle film on DVD with a happy ending – mostly about love and romance, because I was missing David so much and needed some love back in my life.

About three months afterwards, out of the blue, the loss hit me hard. I realized I was facing life alone and I didn't feel up to it. I began to experience severe stress symptoms. If I put music on to break the silence, it felt unbearable – David had listened to music constantly. The television was no help either, as it only seemed to consist of abrasive drama and tragedy. There was no one to talk to or to discuss life's small problems with and the emptiness was frightening.

Another problem had arisen following David's death. I was in financial meltdown. In the period of his long illness, things had been going from bad to worse. It was everything coming together that spurred me to take control and make some hard choices. It was clearly time to act, so I sat down at the kitchen table, on my own, and I developed some ideas that I could – and did – put into practice. This got my life moving again. After all, once I had been a capable person, able to achieve things, so why couldn't I do it again?

The success of my ventures gave me confidence and a renewed identity. I joined an archaeology lecture series, which I had seen advertized in the local newspaper, and it was great fun meeting my fellow students and giving the grey cells a workout again. I even managed to write the required thesis at the end of the course, which was marked highly and increased my faith in myself still further. Having drawn a blank with the bridge tournament that David and I played in each year (no partner!), I signed up for more lectures on art and archaeology at a local museum. There, I met some similarly situated and motivated people of my own age. This was much more reassuring.

It is now nearly two years since David died and I believe I am coming through and out the other side of my grief at last. Looking back, I think it took about nine months to start facing up to my loss and to grieve properly. Yes, I needed to cry – even howl at times – but when the tears dried, I decided to look at life in a new and exciting way. I believed it was important to take practical steps consciously and take responsibility for making myself happy again – even if I didn't believe I would ever by *fully* happy. Although I knew that nothing would ever be the same again, I was now free to find something new to occupy my mind and absorb my energies – and enjoy being able to do exactly what I wanted, when I wanted, without reference or deferring to anyone else at all! I remembered the maxim an old friend of David's gave me: 'Smile, and the world smiles with you! Cry, and you cry alone.'

Thanks to the activities with the lecture group, I have now been lucky enough to meet someone, which has led, most unexpectedly, to new romance in my life. I can hardly believe it, but here I am, after so long, feeling younger and loved again! He has also lost a much-loved wife and we can share our memories of former times without constraint, which we find most therapeutic. It has made me realize that if you do make the effort to deal with difficult circumstances, to be brave and try new things, you are bound to find friendship with the many people who are in the same boat as you, and even embark on a new relationship, if that is what you want and feel is right for you. For me, this relationship does not to replace my beloved late husband, but helps mitigate the inevitable compromises connected with the process of growing old.

Admittedly, at first I was afraid people would not find me interesting, being an aged widow, and that they would be bound to brush me aside in pursuit of their own interests; but I was wrong. Reaching out to people in the same situation as myself made me discover the kindness that is out there, and listening to others' stories had a strongly bonding and cathartic effect.

Of course, you have to meet your domestic responsibilities (such as not letting the house or your routines get in a mess because of neglect), but at the same time, if you have had to complete some unpleasant task, sit down and give yourself a treat; have a glass of wine, or watch a favourite TV programme; cook a more expensive dinner for yourself or buy yourself a nice new piece of clothing! Life is not meant to be all hard work, and I came to realize that as there was no one else to reward me I just had to reward myself! After all, I deserved it, so no need to feel guilty. In this way I was able to hold on to my self-respect, which was so necessary in rebuilding my confidence.

The other thing that I found supported me at the worst times was caring for my two dogs. The fact that they had to be fed and walked at certain times gave a structure to my day, when I would have otherwise felt no need to get up and do anything at all – one of the dangers of a too-solitary existence. The physical exercise and fresh air in my lungs gave me a new perspective on the world in general, and their unconditional friendship was very heartwarming.

I did attend bereavement counseling, too. I must say it was incredibly helpful to hear myself talk and express ideas I was barely aware of. Like the fact that I felt really guilty that I was the one who had been spared to go on living and David was the one who had suffered and died. Like the fact that I had ended up actually wanting him to die, so that neither one of us should have to suffer the agony of his pain and loss any more. Like the fact that I needed the almost unbearable burden, which had lasted seven-and-a-half years, to be lifted from my shoulders at last, before it destroyed me, too. I now know that these are all very natural reactions to a situation you would not wish on your worst enemy, and that I have nothing to be ashamed of − I did my best, when I was needed, and it was good enough.

Now I am able to remember David as he was before the cancer took its dreadful toll; to remember the good times and rejoice in having known him; to remember his enduring sense of humour and wit; his unfailing kindness to others; and his gentle dignity, even in death. I feel able to look forward to a new life, a life for me. One that includes a new relationship without it taking anything away from the love I felt for him. It seems my heart is big enough to hold more than one love, after all!

As we reflected on Margaret's story, we had to acknowledge that there were times in life when we just can't choose what happens to us. Margaret couldn't *choose* David's recovery.

David couldn't *choose* not to die. The choices that Margaret did exercise, however, were made in the context of what was possible. She took charge of her life by focusing on those things that she loved, such as archaeology and history. This proactive approach enabled her to build new friendships and find another life that was meaningful to her.

What interested us in Margaret's story was that in the space created by the loss of her husband, she chose to rebuild her life by focusing on those things that were pleasurable to her. Archaeology and history were nascent interests that had probably been neglected when she was caring for David. We saw them as being similar to muscles that hadn't been used for a long time, and were rather weak and underdeveloped. After David died, she sought to identify these muscles and build their strength, and in doing so, give her life some structure and purpose. None of this replaced her loss, but more of her was brought into the present and she found new possibilities for her life.

# CHAPTER 12

# A Matter of Application – The Technical Stuff!

Making choices can be really exciting. It presents you with the opportunity to tailor your life and to express yourself in a distinctive way. And it enables you to find your own special place in the world. In order to realize your full potential, all you need to start with is the will and the belief that you can make great choices.

The stories in this book provide real examples of how people have made choices that have been important to them. We chose this format because we felt that other's voices would inspire you to develop your ability to choose the life that you want.

Below, we offer a range of ingredients that we hope will stimulate you for this exciting journey. We understand that choices can be threatening and frightening. Indeed, you've read about our storytellers' experiences, and no doubt you have seen the courage that they have displayed in making their choices and the skill they've developed in making sense of them. However, you can't polish a diamond without grit; so you can choose to welcome the grit and know that it's honing you into a gem of a choice maker. Quoting one of our younger storytellers: 'What doesn't kill you makes you stronger.'

The choices we make enable us to live our lives and grow towards true happiness and fulfilment. If we think about the resources at our disposal – the ability to question and reason, the ability to reflect and learn, to read, to write, to look, to listen, to feel pain and joy, to record and memorise, to believe and wonder, to dream and hope – then surely there's a case for us being able to know what is best for ourselves.

## Learning from Experience

For certain, we are all born into different circumstances and we all have unique experiences of being in the world. Although we are born with our parents' genes and grow under their influence, we often don't follow their choices, preferring to make our own and to build our lives as autonomous beings. These choices may be 'good' from a process perspective, meaning that we employed all the best techniques and conferred with all the right people before making them. Their outcomes, however, may be 'bad', suggesting that the quality of the choice is not related to the outcome. How many times have you made a careful choice only to find that it didn't work out as you predicted? This is where some of life's hard lessons are learned – the 'grit' that helps to form the gem. We can choose to see these lessons as 'hard' and we can choose whether or not we learn from them. Herein lies our first major choice.

There are times when life throws up situations where we have no choice – a damaged child, an accident, a crime against property or a person. And there are times when people cast their vote and we can't choose – a broken relationship, the loss of a job, when a child leaves home... and so it goes on. We felt that it would be disingenuous to claim that we have ultimate choice over every aspect of our lives, as plainly, on a practical level, we don't. However, we do have a choice in how we respond and react to these given circumstances. Having said this, we wanted to acknowledge that choice is not a 'black' and 'white' activity, a zero sum game: there are rhythms to the experiences that bring us to our choices. We *need* to grieve when we have experienced a loss, but we can make choices that help us move on from it. Being able to choose does not inevitably mean that we can control our lives and get everything we wish for. Perhaps, all it means is that we can determine how we react to the inevitabilities we encounter.

One of the reasons we feel passionate about this book is because we identified a tendency in people to think that if a choice seems relatively straightforward, it is within their grasp to make it; but if it's a complex or imposed choice, it is either not 'fair' or not possible to take responsibility for it. Life can be hard and present us with extreme situations that make us feel victim to circumstance; yet one of Julie's favourite quotes says that 'even a man in solitary confinement who is unable to hear, speak and see, has the choice of how he thinks and feels.'

As we near the end of the book, we have to ask ourselves the question: what are the common themes that have come from the mouths of the storytellers, and what can we learn from them?

You may remember we acknowledged that everyone has a unique way of learning and adopting new ideas. Firstly, therefore, we are going to place the ideas gleaned from the storytellers in a conceptual framework.

We reflected on the simplicity and complexity of choice; the paradox that is so often the intrinsic challenge of choice-making. What we noticed was that each person picked their way between such a set of opposites and balanced the scale in a way that made sense at the time. Of course, they reserved the right to review their decision from time to time as the consequences of their choice unfolded, but finding dynamic equilibrium seemed to be key to their success. This was most graphically illustrated in *A Matter of Discipline* (Chapter 2), where we heard from two people who understood their choices from opposite ends of the abstinence versus indulgence continuum. We have called this *the extreme continuum,* and you'll find versions of it appearing everywhere! We have illustrated several examples below.

### The Extreme Dream Continuum: 'Big Picture' versus 'Little Picture'

The extreme continuum was particularly clear in Daisy's story, *A Matter of Tomorrow* (Chapter 3), when she described her husband's encouragement to 'just write the essay' as a means of reaching her goal. The co-existence of the 'big picture' and the 'little picture' seems to be a potent way of ensuring that progress is made. Maintaining a tension between immediate tasks with more distant objectives creates meaningful activity on a day-to-day basis. If you think of the times when you felt directionless, and felt you merely existed like a worker bee, you may recall the feelings of frustration it engendered. Similarly, if you reflect on those times that you fantasized about being rich, famous or incredibly successful, but didn't get down to doing anything about it, you may see that being lost in an unrealizable fantasy is equally frustrating. It seems to be true that when broad goals and daily tasks sit alongside each other, it focuses our attention on what needs to be done now in the context of our dreams for the future.

### The Extreme Behavioural Continuum: Abstinence versus Indulgence, Proactive versus Reactive

We have already observed in *A Matter of Discipline*, when we talked about over-eating and smoking, that our two storytellers took up different positions on the continuum of *abstinence* versus *indulgence*. In both cases, finding an accommodation between the two, with some room for movement, seemed to provide a satisfactory way forward that allowed longer-term contentment. Ruby too, in her thoughts about the crisps and the peach in *A Matter of Simplicity* (Chapter 9), unwittingly trod the continuum and decided in favour of a sensible choice somewhere in the middle.

We've also highlighted *proactive* versus *reactive* choices on the extreme behavioural continuum. Proactivity is anticipatory – it begins with taking the first small steps as a result of choosing a course of action. Reactivity, on the other hand, is responsive – it is likely to be prompted by other people or circumstance. Although both behaviours have their place, being proactive allows you to mould and shape your experiences – for good or bad! As you experience yourself being proactive, notice how the energy with which you take action energizes you to take further action. This positive feedback loop enables you to build confidence and become a bolder choice maker.

Remember: not doing something, as a matter of choice, is still doing something.

## The Extreme Decision Making Continuum: Push versus Pull

Often, it is really difficult to stand by and watch people make choices, especially if you can see an obvious decision or solution. It is said that people are unable to help themselves when they 'don't know what they don't know'. Of course this is true, but if they don't find out for themselves, they'll never develop their choice-making muscle. Instead, they'll remain dependent upon others' advice, which runs the risk of being untimely or wrong. Stepping in to help, however well-intentioned and tempting, may be more about our need to rescue someone or to relieve our own discomfort. Being known as a 'wise friend', a 'good advisor' or a 'valuable counsel' is all very well, but it can create a dependency and take away the possibility of learning new skills. When someone doesn't have an answer to a problem, or is unable to make a choice, even though it can be hard to watch, we believe it is important to hold back with suggestions or advice. Instead, we should provide a sympathetic ear, encouraging them to believe in their own potential and find the solution for themselves. This honours and respects their ability to be their own best choice maker, and only then can they enjoy the rewards, both short and long term, of having made a good choice.

We have already talked about the 'push' and 'pull' decisions in Georgina and Lily's stories (*A Matter of Perspective* and *A Matter of Simplicity*). If we can understand the difference between the push/pull dynamic from a personal perspective, we can more easily choose how to assist others and how to help ourselves in making choices.

Having plotted the continua, we then asked ourselves: what can we do about it? In response to this question, we offer you a process – *the spiral*.

## The Spiral

In talking to our storytellers, none of them found making their choices easy. Choosing is not something that we are taught at school, nor is there a one-size-fits-all blueprint for decision making. However, there is a common set of personal qualities and approaches that emerge from the stories; together, we believe, these will provide you with the key to making good choices.

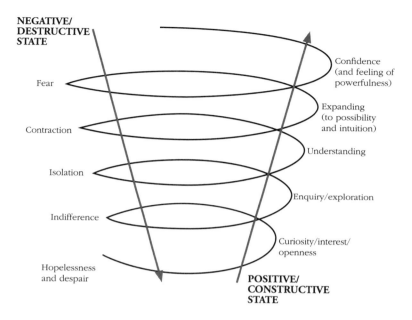

## The Spiral of Choice

To be a confident and skilled choice maker, our storytellers have persistently illustrated that you need to be in a receptive state to enable you to make the best possible decisions. Therefore, we recognize that a framework to illustrate some of the common features of choice-making might be helpful.

We particularly like the spiral because we feel it illustrates the blessings and the curses of choosing and depicts the sequence of feelings that different choices can lead to, whether positive or negative. It also suggests possible remedies if you find yourself heading downwards!

Tracing the righthand arrow with your finger from the bottom to the top, you will see that when you're in a positive state, your curiosity naturally leads you to 'enquiry', which prompts you to seek further facts or information. Here, it is important to delay gratification and not to make an early judgment. Enquiry leads to 'understanding' and on through 'expanding' (i.e., being receptive to new ideas) until you become a confident, powerful choice maker. This *constructive* attitude leads to a virtuous cycle, one that enables you to get into a flow of positivity, leading to decisive, proactive and effective action.

If you trace the lefthand arrow from the top to the bottom, you'll see that when you're in a negative frame of mind, your fear leads you to contract, or shrink, from making choices. Contraction leads to 'isolation' and on through 'indifference' until you fall into hopelessness and despair. This *destructive* attitude leads to a vicious cycle, one that sucks you into a well of negativity. This is a seductive and understandable state. No doubt, we have all been there. Unfortunately, this leads to indecision and feelings of impotence.

You may remember that in our introduction we talked about '...weaving together the gold and silver threads of confidence that will carry us into an autonomous future.' We also suggested that '...choosing gives opportunities for each of us to use qualities in ourselves that may never before have seen the light of day.' These qualities could be the courage to get personal feedback and taking responsibility for gaining clarity. In order to be a great choice maker, we believe that you need to understand and control your own emotional state, ask yourself relevant, challenging questions and be able to design and develop strategies that ensure you make and pursue the choices that are right for you.

The spiral shows in diagrammatic form what needs to be done to cross from a negative to a positive state, as if you were walking over a bridge. You may, however, be wondering how you can develop the inner resources to enable you to make the necessary choices and changes and move from, say, 'contracting' to 'expanding'. The toolkit, containing the spiral (diagnosis), the provocative questions (analysis) and strategies for implementation (solutions), will help you to do this. As with any toolkit, it contains a range of items from which you can pick and choose, depending on your particular circumstances. There is no general formula, only the formula that works for you; and it is up to you to find it from the many permutations of questions, ideas, tips and techniques. This, as you will recall, is not a definitive list, but merely the beginnings of your own list.

It has often been said that we fulfil our own expectations. If we believe that everything will go wrong, it often does! Cynics may say that if you believe the worst, when the worst happens, you're prepared for it. We know, however, through a shift in mindset, it is possible to change one's path by changing one's attitude. We haven't got any examples of pessimism in our stories, which suggests that good choice makers don't dwell in this mindset.

So, if you want to move from an 'I can't' to an 'I can' attitude, the spiral frames the nature of your challenge: that is, to be conscious of how you think and feel your way to a positive mental state. The provocative questions that you'll find in the toolkit will enable you to access more knowledge and understanding as you move through the sequence of the spiral to confident and powerful choices. These fulfil the 'inquisitorial' promise we made to you at the outset.

## Provocative Questions, Timely Choices

Provocative questions, we believe, have tremendous power. There's nothing like a well-aimed question to challenge deeply held assumptions and beliefs! Whether you pick from the list on your own or with a friend, it is helpful to concentrate on the questions as if you'd never heard them before. Often, before someone finishes asking a question (or before we finish reading a question), we anticipate its ending and offer a pre-emptive response. This does not open us to new understanding; it merely reinforces what we think we know. So, we ask that you try to stop yourself from answering the questions automatically, but wait a moment and really be curious about what the question can unearth in you.

Timing is a crucial factor when making precise choices, whatever level of challenge contained therein. So, the 'should' and the 'ought' of choice can end up cutting across a process that is not yet complete and compel us to make a choice prematurely – one that we may regret later. What is that popular saying? 'Act in haste. Repent at leisure'!? So, if you are unable to make what seems like an 'obvious' choice, in spite of the apparent strength of the signals, it may be because the timing is not yet right for you. Alternatively, deeper reflection on what's true for you, and a friend's listening ear, can be what is needed to reveal the subtler truths. Not choosing, then, can be a choice in itself, and this may free you to find the courage of your own convictions.

## Three Circles of Questions

In the three concentric circles (see diagram on page 180), you will find some pertinent questions that will help you in your choice-making. They are not exhaustive, but they may stimulate your creative juices! The questions fall into three categories, which are designed to tap into your thoughts and feelings about the choices you're making. Notice the responses they evoke in you.

We have placed the more reflective questions in the central circle. These are the 'big' questions that lie at the root of your choices, and will help you crystallize your dreams and aspirations. They may be difficult to answer but it is worth reflecting on them honestly and courageously, as they are the foundation stone of your future actions.

The questions in the second circle will encourage you to take another perspective and deepen your self-understanding. You can also use these to challenge your mindset and examine your choices from different angles.

The practical questions have been placed in the outer circle. You may want to move in and out of the circles to complete your scrutiny and ensure that you have identified the desires and aspirations that are most meaningful to you. We are asking you to trust this process, as it allows you to hear your inner voice, tap into your wisdom and discover what to do. Don't forget to record your responses. This will ensure they are remembered and become concrete.

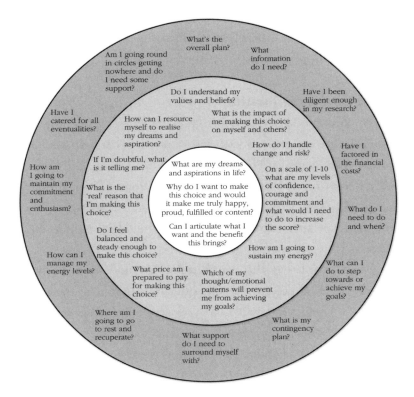

## Three Circles of Questions

Having come full circle, it is now time for us to hand you, the reader, the matter of choice. We hope that you are feeling inspired and eager to use the thoughts and ideas that we, and all our storytellers, have given you. We believe that you have all the answers inside you and that all you need to do is bring them into the light of day and trust your own judgment. You are your own oracle.

Once you become adept at asking yourself the 'right' questions and finding the courage to answer them honestly, you will become the best person to make choices for yourself. In doing so, you will be in the driving seat of your own life, consciously taking yourself where you really want to go, warts and all!

Remember that every choice you make, no matter how small, defines the person you are; so keep choosing and show your colours in all their depth and subtlety.

We wish you well in your choosing.

CHAPTER 13
# A Matter for Reflection

We have found writing this book together both an amazing and unexpected experience. *Amazing* because in our collaboration and friendship we discovered the beauty of compromise without the feeling of loss. *Unexpected* because we have entered territory that has given rise to many changes for us, both personally and professionally.

Writing *A Matter of Choice* has been life changing. As we worked within the confines of a deadline, everything became accentuated and our choices became more visible, more important and more conscious. Of course, we were not alone in our adventure. Our storytellers have shared their experiences, their insights and their wisdom through the nine months' gestation period that grew this book and readied it for the light of day. We are intensely appreciative of them and the world they opened up to us.

The power of making deliberate choices and the power of being present and attending to what's happening 'right now' are the two most significant lessons to have emerged from writing this book. We also learnt the importance of being clear and confident about what you want to do and how you want to live your life. Having read the extraordinary stories of courage and determination related by our storytellers, we believe that almost anything is possible through full awareness and clear focus.

Once you are conscious of it, choices appear everywhere! We have come to see the world through the prism of choice. It seems there are very few instances when a decision does not involve making a choice – even when it appears, on first sight, not to be so. So, here we are, a couple of 'choice-aholics'! And we cannot stress enough our gratitude in becoming so.

*Dena Michelli and Julie Simpson*

# APPENDIX

Not only have our storytellers shared the choices they have made, often in difficult circumstances, but also they have given us an insight into the resources and ideas they drew from. We hope these will help you to make your choices, as it did them; and we encourage you, again, to add to the list so that your toolkit will be well stocked with options.

Some of these ideas may not resonate with you instantly or suit your inclinations; however, in the spirit of openness, we'd like to encourage you to try something new and be receptive to the benefits that others have derived from these ideas.

Remember, one of the requisites of a good choice maker is to feel in a positive state of mind. When your emotions are heightened, it is impossible for you to allow other stimuli or information to enter your thoughts and feelings. Many of these tips and techniques will help you reach a balanced state that favours good choice.

| TIPS AND TECHNIQUES<br>These gifts were given by our storytellers – you may want to put some of them in your toolkit | CHAPTER AND MAIN OUTPUT |
|---|---|
| When trying to let go of the habit of over-eating, Judy focused on what was important, like her interests and her circle of friends. Her first suggestion was to decide what is most important to you. Judy also commented that when her energy levels were low, she was more susceptible to the sweet foods and chocolates that she believed would plug the energy gap. Instead of falling into this trap, however, she chose to go to bed, or engage in some form of relaxation. This is her suggestion to you. | **Chapter 2:**<br>**A Matter of**<br>**Discipline**<br><br>**You can choose**<br>**what you want**<br>**to choose** |
| When trying to beat her smoking habit, Maya said she'd recommend getting proper support in giving up, as well as thinking about the consequences if you didn't conquer your habit. This can reinforce your commitment. | |
| Angela, when parting from her fiancé, said: 'Don't lose your sense of self.' She suggested you challenge the logical voice in your head and listen for the quieter voice that is your gut instinct – and keep reinforcing what you really want.<br><br>Daisy, when working for her Masters degree, was helped by remembering why she was studying, while at the same time, focusing on the task in hand. She found it helpful to build a file of jobs that appealed to her. This helped her be more precise about the choices she was seeking to make. Also, she suggested, do your research. The internet can be quite confusing, but it can be a great way of seeing what's out there; whatever decision or choice you're thinking of making, find out as much as you can about it. | **Chapter 3:**<br>**A Matter of**<br>**Tomorrow**<br><br>**Live life for**<br>**yourself** |

When Mike was trying to let go of an old resentment, he challenged himself by asking: 'What's the point of holding on?' Mike was able to challenge himself by running an equation through his mind, weighing in favour of his self-esteem and not losing himself to the unproductive negative feelings he felt. He also used humour to get things into proportion – after all, we must be able to laugh at life! And he advocated depersonalising what you may perceive to be actions against you – particularly if it is by an organization. If we can depersonalise something, we may then be able to look at it more rationally, rather than emotionally.

James, describing the process of 'letting go', recommended meditation to silence the constant chatter that prevents you from listening to yourself.

**Chapter 4:**
**A Matter of**
**Letting Go**

**Use your energy**
**for vital things**

---

Roseanna dealt with a situation she had not chosen. She made choices by reframing how she thought about her situation. She also tried to see the ridiculous side of her life, but was careful to make a risk assessment in order to keep herself, and others, safe.

Mary turned towards her passions, which drew her focus into productive activity.

**Chapter 5:**
**A Matter of**
**Acceptance**

**Choose the lens**
**through which**
**you look at life**

---

Melanie offered several tools. Ask for what you need. Take up new interests that can be done to suit your daily rhythm, such as tapestry, reading and writing. You may want to start a journal and write everything down – words can be incredibly therapeutic. She also suggested venturing out to 'safe' places where you won't encounter people who might try to invade your privacy.

Barbara suggested taking time away from others to allow yourself to hear what is going on within. She recommends time and space alone to do some connecting with your inner voice. In practical terms, she spends time walking in the countryside, gardening or sitting and looking at a nice view.

**Chapter 6:**
**A Matter of the**
**Unexpected**

**Trust your own**
**judgment**

| | |
|---|---|
| Georgina asked: 'Was this the right choice?' This is a provocative question that allowed her to engage in work that had purpose and meaning, enabling her to establish her identity. She also advised that people examine their values and put them at the centre of the decision making equation.<br><br>In weighing up her decision, Sarah did not allow her heart to rule her head. There are always negative effects to any decision, and any course you take will have highs and lows. The best you can do is look for the positives and don't beat yourself up. | **Chapter 7:**<br>**A Matter of**<br>**Perspective**<br><br>**Good is good**<br>**enough** |
| Mark analysed his situation and came to a realistic conclusion after asking himself the question: 'What would happen if I chose the alternative route?'<br><br>Emma talked of not being influenced by others' judgements, listening to yourself and challenging the feelings of 'guilt' that you may feel as you make your choice against the majority view. She suggests that we question the foundation upon which this guilt is built, as it is not a fruitful feeling.<br><br>Jessica, in choosing her work, wrote stories about her life, which enabled her to identify themes of personal and professional importance. This gave her a real sense of who she was and what she was best suited to. Practicing self-assertion, she recommended being open to change, making your own decisions and being strong enough to admit your mistakes. | **Chapter 8:**<br>**A Matter of**<br>**Purpose**<br><br>**Do the things you**<br>**love to do** |
| Lily emphasised that if it doesn't kill you, it will make you stronger. So if you want to do something, 'Just do it!' Don't go through life thinking, 'I wish I'd done that'. If your choice doesn't turn out as you wanted, at least you've tried. Regret is the worst thing!<br><br>Ruby suggested that all choices matter, big or small, because they affect your whole life in the long term. She always tries to think positively and be brave about her choices. | **Chapter 9:**<br>**A Matter of**<br>**Simplicity**<br><br>**Just do it!** |

| | |
|---|---|
| Margaret suggested making a plan and treating yourself. The plan needs to include people – both new and familiar, and activities – things you love to do, and things you may be interested in doing for the first time. Make sure you deal with your immediate, practical concerns and continue with your routines. When work is out of the way, give yourself a treat. I think it's so important when on your own to be kind to yourself: seek the company of people who will listen to you; enjoy your pets; and be active and fill your lungs with fresh air. | **Chapter 10: A Matter of Recovery**<br><br>**Know the 'point of choice'** |
| Jane advocated being honest with yourself, choosing friends carefully and getting support. | **Chapter 11: A Matter of New Beginnings**<br><br>**Life is for living** |

## Tips: A Quick Guide

In conclusion, we want to highlight the frequently mentioned tips, which we think are so important in becoming a great choice maker.

- Firstly, remember that you are a unique individual. Trust your inner resources and let your beliefs, values and passions inform your decisions.
- Secondly, find people or a group who will be supportive of you and not judgmental. No matter what choice you are making, speaking of it to others whilst they *really* listen to you can be both affirming and revealing. Although you may feel vulnerable at first, sharing your thoughts will help you see and make sense of your own reality. This is *so* important.

- Thirdly, visualize and commit to your goals, keeping them at the forefront of your mind. This will enable you to prioritize and make sense of the time and energy you spend in performing the tasks that will get you there.

Finally, we believe:

**You can be anything you want if you give up the belief that you can't!**

# ABOUT THE AUTHORS

Dena has pursued a three-pronged career. She began her professional life as a mechanical engineer before moving into a business development role for a prominent university business school. Preferring to be in the heart of the learning arena, she completed her PhD on transformative learning and now facilitates personal growth as an international executive coach and writer. Dena makes medieval style stained glass windows to refresh her creativity – mainly for friends and family.

Julie's career has been through several iterations. She started her working life at a well-known clothing retail store where she took responsibility for growing the talent of people in the organisation. She built on these skills in a consulting role whilst training to be a person-centred therapist using Rogerian principles. These formed the backbone of her coaching practice, which she has developed in the international arena, travelling widely and working with senior leaders. Julie has a passion and skill for natural horsemanship and puts this to use with her three horses.